KOBE BRYANT

LAKER FOR LIFE

Copyright © 2016 Los Angeles News Group

No part of this publication may be reproduced, stored in a retrieval system, or transmitted in any form by any means, electronic, mechanical, photocopying, or otherwise, without prior written permission of the publisher, Triumph Books LLC, 814 North Franklin Street; Chicago, Illinois 60610.

This book is available in quantity at special discounts for your group or organization.
For further information, contact:

Triumph Books LLC
814 North Franklin Street
Chicago, Illinois 60610
Phone: (312) 337-0747
www.triumphbooks.com

Printed in U.S.A.
ISBN: 978-1-62937-340-9

Los Angeles News Group
Ron Hasse, Publisher
Bill Van Laningham, Vice President, Marketing
Frank Pine, Executive Editor
Tom Moore, Executive Sports Editor
Dean Musgrove, Photo Editor

Content packaged by Mojo Media, Inc.
Joe Funk: Editor
Jason Hinman: Creative Director

Front cover photo by San Gabriel Valley Tribune: Keith Birmingham
Back cover photo by L.A. Daily News: Hans Gutknecht

This is an unofficial publication. This book is in no way affiliated with, licensed by, or endorsed by Kobe Bryant, the National Basketball Association or the Los Angeles Lakers.

L.A. Daily News: Hans Gutknecht

CONTENTS

Introduction

Mark Heisler

I met Kobe Bryant two months shy of his 18th birthday in Chicago in 1996, where he was attending the NBA pre-draft camp. He was all by himself on the mezzanine of the Marriott Hotel in the Loop, staring wistfully down into the lobby like a teenage boy a long way from home.

So I was wrong about Kobe from my very first impression.

He wasn't overwhelmed in the least. Innocent as he looked, he was like a crown prince perusing a world he felt born to rule.

Given his up-front ambition to surpass Michael Jordan, a long line of people were wrong about Kobe — essentially everyone who ever heard of him aside from immediate family.

Perhaps half the little boys in the nation born after 1975, and a significant percentage in the world, set out to be like Mike, although few announced their intentions as Kobe did. None of them made it. Only Kobe came close.

The rest of those boys only had dreams. Kobe had a destiny.

Well, he thought he did, anyway. He realized is at age six, he would tell me years later.

Precocious as he was, everyone tried to let him down easy. In the Philadelphia summer league he grew up playing in between his father's seasons in Italy, founder Sonny Hill made all the players attend instructional sessions in which it was hammered into the heads of the players, all of whom dreamed of playing in the NBA what a long shot it would be.

The kids were supposed to list realistic ambitions for when the dreams faded. Kobe wouldn't. He was going to play in the NBA, period.

Teenagers had already begun coming straight to the NBA from high school. Kevin Garnett had done it the year before but they were all young bigs.

Kobe was a shooting guard — "Grant Hill with a jump shot" according to his prep rep. The world wasn't ready for 17-year-old, 6-5, 165-pound NBA rookies.

"He's kidding himself," said NBA scouting director Marty Blake, an old league hand whose job was to tell the press nice things about prospects. "Sure, he'd like to come out. I'd like to be a movie star. He's not ready."

I was ideally suited to cover Kobe. I had covered his father, the happy-go-lucky former player known in Philadelphia as "Jellybean" which was why Kobe's middle name is "Bean."

I was friendly with Kobe's paternal grandfather, another happy-go-lucky guy everyone called "Big Joe" from summer league. I remember seeing Joe and Pam Cox, Kobe's mom, before they got married, when they

Kobe Bryant celebrates after hitting a three pointer in the fourth quarter, as the Lakers beat the Jazz 119-109 during Game 2 of a first round Western Conference match-up in 2009. (San Gabriel Valley Tribune: Keith Birmingham)

were just kids on a date in the Palestra.

I was one of the few press people Kobe let get close for his first eight seasons. Then I wrote something he didn't like and got stoney looks for eight years or so, although he was professional enough to take my questions in interview sessions.

He chilled in recent seasons. Now with the fans who scorned him around the NBA realizing how much they would miss him, Kobe, enchanted by the love, is like blood brothers with the few of us left from the beginning.

If no one dreamed it would end this way, it should. There were players almost as good as Kobe and a whole lot more fundamental but no one put as much into the game as he did, training year-round in a way that not even demon workers like Magic Johnson had.

I've covered a lot of cool people, many of whom were a lot easier to deal with, who did a lot of cool things. Nothing matches my 20 years watching Kobe go from this quiet young guy to an all-time NBA great.

Just like he said he would. That's Kobe Bryant.

This is Kobe at 21: We're in the bleachers at the practice site early in the 1999-2000 season. His struggle of with Shaquille O'Neal has begun to emerge. The new coach, Phil Jackson, isn't having it. The ball will go into Shaq first, period.

"So," I tell Kobe, ever helpful, "this shot where you dribble the ball up and then shoot it is no good."

In person, if not in games, Kobe is well-mannered and soft-voiced, still pretty reserved.

"Why?" he says.

"Well, maybe next time down, you run a back door and Rick Fox sees you're open and says, 'Bleep you.'"

Kobe seems surprised that Fox would ever react like that.

Kobe was like that. I interviewed him a lot but quoted him rarely, which is the way he preferred it. He often played dumb to see if you had a point that you could explain.

For years when I thought back to this exchange, I thought Kobe knew exactly what I was saying and why. Now I'm not sure.

Kobe was so bulletproof, he may have thought that it was OK for him, being Kobe, to take a 20-footer before anyone passed to anyone else, and that Fox believed it as much as he did.

Michael Jordan grew up trying unsuccessfully to beat two older brothers.

Kobe was raised a godling as the youngest child, and only boy, by loving parents and two older sisters.

Even after becoming the star of stars, Jordan mused privately about being pulled off his pedestal. I don't think that ever came up for Kobe.

Kobe would have been a better player, and would have taken fewer awful shots if he had some fear but he had as little as God allows.

That's what covering him was like, 20 years of marveling at him.

It's the 1998 All-Star Game in New York. The youth of America has voted Kobe to the first team even though he doesn't start for the Lakers.

NBC goes off its rocker, promoting it as a shootout between Kobe, 19, and Michael, 35, who's about to become a six-time champion and five-time MVP.

Rising to the occasion — and waving the grownups out of his way until West teammate Karl Malone takes himself out — Kobe shoots nine of the first 11 times he touches the ball.

I mention it to Laker publicist Raymond Ridder, sitting next to me.

"That's two less than he shot it in the rookie game last year," says Raymond without missing a beat.

Of course, perfect ambition means no one ever set himself up the way Kobe did.

At 23 he was a three-time NBA champion and a four-time All-Star.

At 24 he was on trial for sexual assault, a charge that would ultimately be dropped and settled.

At 25, he was on his own after the Lakers traded O'Neal to keep him, reducing themselves to also-rans, while players around the league sided with Shaq against Kobe.

At 27 Kobe lamented his existence in a first-person magazine article, wondering if he would ever win another title — and, for the first time, questioning the goals he had set for himself.

"Am I supposed to obsess myself with winning only to win, retire and wonder if all my sacrifices were worth it?" he wrote.

"Is it OK for me to sacrifice time away from my children, time watching them grow up, missing Easter, Christmas and other special moments, to win a ring?"

It was as if his soul has been burned to the consistency of charcoal. He was a total pain with the local press corps which referred to him sardonically as "Ocho," Spanish for eight, his original number eight.

One night he overheard a writer ask Lamar Odom a question.

"Oh," said Kobe, assuming, of course, someone was trying to pull something over on Odom, "the old okeydoke, huh?"

Lots of people got The Glare. He stared referees down so intently, you thought he might melt one.

At 28 he hit bottom, demanding to be traded, calling owner Jerry Buss "a liar" and slamming GM Mitch Kupchak

At 29 he was the MVP as the Lakers acquired Pau Gasol and made the first of three Finals in a row.

At 31 he was a five-time champion.

So, it wasn't a setup, after all. It was greatness his many critics would have to acknowledge.

I saw Kobe the other night in the Laker dressing room before a game.

I was over in a corner, chatting with Baxter Holmes of ESPN. Kobe, who wasn't playing, came out of the trainer's room, heading in the other direction for the players' lounge.

He turned, saw me, waved, then stopped and came over.

We chatted for a minute. I told him how happy I was to see him get all he was getting because no one deserved it more.

He said, "Thank you," wearing this embarrassed smile that we never saw much of, or never saw, before this season.

That's Kobe Bryant.

Thanks for the adventure of a lifetime, for all of us. ∎

Mark Heisler
March 15, 2016

Mark Heisler has written an NBA column since 1991 and was honored with the Naismith Hall of Fame's Curt Gowdy Award in 2006. His column is published Sundays in Los Angeles News Group print editions.

Bryant Might Be a Laker

Divac Could Be Hornet If Likely Deal Comes Off

By Marc Stein • June 27, 1996

Kobe Bryant, from high school to the Lakers? That was the tantalizing prospect that had Jerry West and Del Harris struggling to mask their giddiness late Wednesday night, after the Charlotte Hornets took the 17-year-old wunderkind with the 13th pick in the NBA Draft and then announced that they'd be trading him.

Inglewood immediately surfaced as the probable destination for Bryant, who would likely force West to part with starting center Vlade Divac.

"They've made him available and we told them that we're interested," said the Lakers' executive vice president, who for now has nothing more than Arkansas-Little Rock point guard Derek Fisher, the No. 24 overall selection, from the draft proceedings in New Jersey.

"We're definitely interested, but we do not have a deal at this point."

The tone of West's and, later, coach Harris' voice suggested that the Lakers do expect a deal at some point, if not this week then shortly after the salary cap rises to $24.3 million on July 1.

Given West's intense fondness for the Pennsylvania prep star — management privately maintains that Bryant has more talent than anyone on the present roster — it's difficult to imagine him letting another team swoop in and nab the 6-foot-6, 200-pound swingman.

That's even if the price tag is Divac, a definite risk since the Lakers have no guarantee they can sign free agent-to-be Shaquille O'Neal or re-sign Elden Campbell.

"I was impressed more than I can say," Harris recalled of Bryant's workout at the Forum two weeks earlier. "It was really stunning to see what he could do as a 17-year-old man."

Just when it seemed that all the pre-draft speculation about a trade involving Divac and No. 4 overall pick Stephon Marbury was just talk, and just as it appeared that the Lakers would wind up spending a mostly quiet evening in their war room securing Fisher late in the first round, word spread of Bryant's availability.

Hornets vice president Bob Bass then revealed that he has been talking with an unspecified team — believed to be the Lakers — all week in hopes of giving new coach Dave Cowens the big man Charlotte lacks.

"This was our No. 1 thing to happen," Bass said of drafting Bryant and then shopping him. "We started talking about it Monday and kept talking about it, but there was no deal if the guy they want wasn't there. Bryant had to be there."

To bring him to Los Angeles, the Lakers will probably have to wait until Monday, when, barring

Kobe had an incredible prep career at Lower Merion High School, including a senior year in which he was named Naismith High School Player of the Year, Gatorade Men's National Basketball Player of the Year, a McDonald's All-American, and a USA Today All-USA First Team player. (AP Images)

"We don't see many kids who are 17 years old and can do the things he can do." —Jerry West

a lockout, the Hornets will be able to renounce free-agent guard Kenny Anderson to make room for Divac's $4,137,000 salary for 1996-97.

It is not known whether the Hornets are aware of Divac's hints at retirement if he is traded away. Sources close to the seven-year veteran, who is in the former Yugoslavia practicing for the Summer Olympics, told the *Daily News* this week that Divac is adamant about keeping his family in Los Angeles and prepared to walk away from the game at 28.

Charlotte has showed interest in Divac in the past, most recently in November before sending Alonzo Mourning to Miami.

West was unwilling to give up Divac then but sees Bryant, the son of longtime NBA forward Joe "Jellybean" Bryant, as "a potential NBA star."

"We don't see many kids who are 17 years old and can do the things he can do," West said.

Bryant, indeed, is a unique prospect, unlike any of the other 36 underclassmen available in Wednesday's draft or even Minnesota's Kevin Garnett, last year's preps-to-the-pros sensation.

Bryant — who, according to Harris, has three-position capability in the mold of Eddie Jones — speaks fluent Italian and could have attended the university of his choice after scoring 1,080 on the Scholastic Assessment Test.

He chose instead to bypass college and turn pro and, if he comes to the Lakers, would give Harris the privilege of coaching his first father-and-son tandem. Joe Bryant played for Harris in Houston.

"This would be the first time I coached a father and son in the NBA ... if it happens," Harris said with a smile.

If it happens, Bryant will cost the Lakers $845,800 for his first season based on the NBA's rookie salary cap. Combined with the $509,600 that Fisher would receive and the $4 million-plus going to Charlotte if Divac is involved, the Lakers will be gaining nearly $2.8 million in cap room to add to the $6-9 million they've reserved for the pursuit of O'Neal.

Whether or not it happens, the Lakers do think they have solidified their backcourt picture with the acquisition of Fisher, a 6-1, 200-pound left-hander who is a natural point guard — unlike Sedale Threatt, a free agent who isn't expected back, and Frankie King, last year's second-round pick.

Fisher, who averaged 14.6 points and 5.1 assists as a senior, was one of 14 players the Lakers looked at in workouts and one of three names they were interested in most. Alabama's Roy Rogers was gone by the time L.A. selected; two slots later, West decided to take Fisher over Georgetown forward Jerome Williams.

"We hope that he'll be able to come in and, frankly, play right away," West said. ■

Kobe Bryant, 17, jokes with the media as he holds his Los Angeles Lakers jersey during a news conference in July, 1996. Bryant was acquired from the Charlotte Hornets by the Lakers in exchange for veteran center Vlade Divac. (AP Images)

Lakers' Teenager Grows Up

19-Years-Old, 100% Basketball

By Doug Krikorian • Feburary 3, 1998

At 19, you're hanging with pals, carrying a phony ID, hitting the books, rushing a fraternity, holding down a job, engaging in romance, trying to figure what direction to pursue in life.

At 19, you're unaware of the cruel twists that lie ahead because of being shielded so long in a cocoon of youth and its seemingly endless glad tomorrows and you think you know more than you do.

At 19, you're brimming with energy and hope for a bright future and the wallet you carry seldom has much money in it.

Kobe Bryant, the Lakers' 19-year-old prodigy, makes a mockery out of such stereotypes.

For one thing, he's already a millionaire whose course in upcoming years is set.

For another, he's a refreshingly self-effacing person who understands that his modest years conspire against his knowing everything.

For still another, he's not interested in the nightclub scene, or frat parties, or academic studies, or driving around with buddies checking out the sights that so entrance others of his age group.

"What are you going to do tonight?" I asked Kobe Bryant Sunday afternoon after he had scored 20 points in helping the Lakers to their 112-87 impalement of the Chicago Bulls.

"Oh, I'll go home and watch a tape of this game," replied Bryant, seated in front of his dressing cubicle in the Lakers' locker room. "I'll analyze the mistakes I made. I'll see what I could have done better. I might watch it a couple of times."

"You're not going to go out with friends and have a good time?" I persisted to Bryant.

"Oh, no, I don't do that," said Bryant. "I spend most of the time at my house with my family. I might go to movies once in a while. But my life is almost 100 percent basketball."

As you might know, Kobe Bryant is not your typical teenager.

Few his age are 6-7. None inspire comparisons to Michael Jordan. None become starters in the NBA All-Star game. And none act during interviews with a poise and maturity that belie their years.

And I can't think of any other teenager in American athletics who's become a more revered figure than Kobe Bryant.

Indeed, at the moment, on a Laker team that includes a legitimate superstar in Shaquille O'Neal and other exceptional performers like Nick Van Exel

Kobe soars to the basket in a January, 1997 game against the Detroit Pistons. The Lakers brought him along slowly during his rookie season, starting only six of 71 games he played. (AP Photo)

and Eddie Jones, Kobe Bryant just might be the most popular player.

At least he receives the loudest cheers at the Forum.

And kids around Los Angeles — as well as around the country — have come to hero-worship this appealing young man who so enamored Jerry West in high school that West was willing to trade Vlade Divac to Charlotte for Bryant's drafting rights.

"What are your feelings about becoming such a favorite among so many young fans?" I asked Bryant.

"I think it's really cool," he said. "I love kids myself. I feel very comfortable around them. Hey, I'm still a kid myself. I think one reason a lot of the kids like me is that they can relate to me. I think a lot of the kids cheering for me these days are people only four, five, six years younger than me.

"I guess it's an added responsibility for me to be looked up to, but I'll take it. It doesn't bother me a bit. I'll just continue to try to be myself."

While Kobe Bryant is faultless in his dealings with the media, he still admittedly has his rough edges on the hardwoods.

Oh, he has been an explosive performer this season off the bench for the Lakers averaging more than 17 points a game, but he can have undisciplined periods as he did during the first half against the Bulls when he kept taking off-balanced, hurried shots in a wild display that was maddening to both his teammates and his coach, Del Harris.

"Kobe was trying to do a little too much in the early stages against the Bulls," said Harris. "I pulled him aside and told him, 'Slow down a little, Kobe, and let it come to you.' And he did. And, man, once he did he was fun to watch. You just marvel at his ability."

"I sometimes let my emotions dictate my play — and that's when I play poorly as I did early against the Bulls," said Bryant. "I'd been waiting for this game a long time, and I

The rookie Bryant is heckled by teammates as a television cameraman adjusts a microphone on his jersey for an interview during the Lakers Media Day in October, 1996. (AP Images)

was just a little too nervous and excited. You always want to prove yourself against the best — and the Bulls and Michael Jordan are the best. I was just too impatient."

"What aspect of your game do you feel you have to improve in most?" I wondered.

"Every aspect," he replied. "Shooting, defending, passing, positioning. Everything. In order to become the best, you have to keep improving all the time. And that's my goal. Just to keep improving."

"What do you learn from playing against Michael Jordan?"

"What I learn from Michael is the way he uses his teammates, the way he sets them up with his passes. I've still got a lot to learn in this area. I've got a lot to learn in all areas."

No doubt Kobe Bryant does.

He at times looks like a 19-year-old who would have been wiser to have learned his trade in college.

But other times he looks like he's on the threshold of succeeding Michael Jordan as the NBA's marquee attraction.

"I'm really looking forward to the NBA All-Star game next Sunday," said Bryant with wide-eyed anticipation. "That's just going to be great — Madison Square Garden, those great fans, competing against the best in the NBA. I just can't wait."

"Do you ever think how it would have been for you had you decided to attend college?" I asked.

Kobe Bryant paused momentarily, and then a soft grin covered his face.

"Yeah, once in a while it crosses my mind," he finally replied. "But not often. I took a three-unit course last summer at UCLA, and it was really difficult. The only course I'm taking right now is basketball. NBA 101." ∎

Right: Kobe's game was in the early stages of development during his rookie year but his elite athleticism was immediately breathtaking. (AP Images) Opposite: Kobe Bryant passes to a teammate under the basket as Houston Rockets, Sam Mack (5) and Othella Harrington (32) look on during a March, 1997 game. (AP Images)

Hoop-L.A.!

Lakers Beat Pacers for NBA Title

By Steve Dilbeck · June 20, 2000

A promise delivered, a moment to savor, a time to celebrate.

An NBA championship in hand.

Twelve years after they captured the last title of the Showtime era, a very different group defeated the stubborn Indiana Pacers, 116-111, on Monday night to bring the Lakers their seventh title in the L.A. franchise history.

One-year after the gray-haired Phil Jackson — the Zen-speaking mystic of bottomless calm — was hired to lead the Lakers back from a season of turmoil to the pinnacle of the NBA, the Lakers ended the best-of-seven series in six games.

"The first of many — just like it was before," said Lakers owner Jerry Buss.

The title follows an empty decade for L.A. professional championships and a troubled era for the city as well.

It is the first pro title for the City of Angels since the Lakers and Dodgers both captured championships in 1988.

This one was marked by the flash and dare of guard Kobe Bryant and the power and thunder of Most Valuable Player Shaquille O'Neal, a combination of style and substance that other teams challenged, but ultimately no one could match.

When the tense game, led by the Pacers most of the way, finally ended, O'Neal could not hold his emotions in check. Tears streamed down his cheeks.

Then, Bryant leaped into his arms; O'Neal next searched out his mother, embracing her with his giant arms.

"I've held my emotions for almost 11 years," O'Neal said.

"Three years in college, eight years in the pros. I always wanted to win. It just came out. I'm happy for L.A. It's a great moment."

The Lakers were this man-child throughout the postseason, a young but talented team with its core of O'Neal and Bryant straining mightily to take the crown.

They would look dynamic one night, a maturing team reaching for the basketball heavens. And then they would come back to disappoint, the sheepish child knowing it had failed to live up to expectations, if even its own.

Six times, an NBA postseason record, they failed to close out a series. They seemed determined to find the difficult path, to tantalize their fans before reaching their greatness.

In the end, no amount of growing pains would stop

Kobe Bryant celebrates the first of five titles with the Lakers from a double-decker open top bus during the 2000 championship parade. (L.A. Daily News: Charlotte Schmid-Maybach)

their ascent to the NBA summit.

"This is the best feeling in the world," said Lakers forward Glen Rice.

The Pacers made the Lakers earn their title Monday, pushing them hard and forcing them to dig deep to pull out the title game.

The Pacers led throughout most of the contest, still firing away from beyond the 3-point line and threatening to force a decisive Game 7.

O'Neal, who duplicated his regular-season and All-Star MVP triumphs, took command in the fourth quarter, scoring 13 of his game-high 41 points.

With the score tied at 103 with 5:04 to play after a seven-point Pacers run, the Lakers connected on consecutive baskets by Robert Horry, O'Neal and Bryant.

They had a lead they would cling to until the final buzzer sounded.

Gold and purple streamers and confetti fell from the ceiling, "I Love L.A." blared and the celebration began.

The championship validated the coaching greatness of Jackson, who after winning six titles with the Chicago Bulls, captured a championship in his first season with the Lakers. He and Alex Hannum are the only coaches in the NBA's 52-year history to win titles with two different teams.

It was a grand confirmation for team Executive Vice President Jerry West, who nine years after the Lakers last made it to the NBA Finals, pieced together an entirely new team to earn his sixth title as a Lakers executive.

It was another reason to party for Buss; for veterans Rice, Ron Harper, A.C. Green, Brian Shaw and John Salley to feel young; for the 21-year-old Bryant to feel his star rise; and for O'Neal to establish himself as the most imposing force in the NBA.

It was even partial redemption for the brand new Staples Center, maligned for its sterile and subdued environment.

The Lakers clinched each of their four playoff series at home, and Monday it rocked like never before.

"What a start for the Staples Center," Jackson said. "What a start for the new millennium."

The Lakers first exerted their dominance in the regular season, rolling to a league-best 67-15 mark. The playoffs offered a wild ride.

Most people are still trying to figure out how they won Game 7 of the Western Conference Finals, a game that saw them overcome a 15-point fourth-quarter deficit.

"They had a miracle game, seventh game against Portland," Jackson said.

In the closing moments of Monday's game, as Bryant walked to the bench, he held up his left hand to the crowd and pointed to its ring finger.

"That's one ring," Bryant said. "We did it for ourselves. We did it for Los Angeles, because they deserved it. It's been a long drought." ■

Kobe defends Indiana Pacers guard Mark Jackson during Game 1 of the 2000 NBA Finals. He averaged 15.6 points per game in the Lakers 4-2 series win. (L.A. Daily News: Gus Ruelas)

Twice as Nice!

Lakers Beat Sixers, Launch Dynasty with 2nd Title

By Karen Crouse • June 16, 2001

PHILADELPHIA—Just how good are these Lakers?

They have a chance to become the New York Yankees of the NBA . The Tiger Woods of basketball. The benchmark by which every other franchise is measured.

A dynasty.

The Lakers beat the Philadelphia 76ers 108-96 at the First Union Center on Friday night to close out the best-of-seven series 4-1 and complete a historic 15-1 run made all the more remarkable by the fact the Lakers managed not to lose a single postseason game on enemy turf.

The Lakers' march to a second consecutive world championship was so sweeping, so methodical, so merciless, it has left the NBA landscape scorched.

This dynasty should be around awhile.

"I never told anybody this," said forward Rick Fox, "but Kobe (Bryant) sat with me four years ago and said, 'I'm going to win 10 championships.'"

Fox laughed at the memory.

"I looked at him and said, this kid has confidence. But now I'm thinking, I need to listen to the cat."

Shaquille O'Neal, named the series MVP after averaging 33 points and 15.8 rebounds, wasted few words in describing the Lakers' achievement: "I think it was just us looking for an identity. And we found it."

He has promised to go on "a power diet" over the summer, the better to report to training camp leaner than last fall when he showed up looking conspicuously like The Big Jelly Doughnut.

At this point, O'Neal's appetite is probably the only thing that can slow him. Sixers center Dikembe Mutombo certainly couldn't slow him despite playing some of the finest basketball of his 10-year pro career.

"He's not dominating Dikembe, he's dominating our team," Sixers backup center Matt Geiger said on the eve of O'Neal's 29-point, 13-rebound romp in Game 5. "I don't know of anybody I've ever seen, (Michael) Jordan included, that has single-handedly dominated the game the way Shaq is. He's playing better than he ever has."

Those are weighty words considering O'Neal was the MVP of the regular season and the Finals last year.

As the Lakers stretched their lead to an unreachable 17 points early in the fourth quarter, we saw the hollowed expressions of forward Tyrone Hill and guard Aaron McKie.

The Lakers raided the Sixers' building, turning the festival atmosphere inside the First Union Center into a funeral. When Mutombo fouled out with less than four minutes remaining, Sixers coach Larry Brown had the

Bryant hypes up the Lakers crowd at the celebration of their 2001 NBA Finals triumph over the 76ers. (L.A. Daily News: David Sprague)

vacant stare of a man looking past the court, into the crystal ball that divines his future.

Brown has talked of retiring. Now would appear to be as good a time as any. Better to walk away on his own terms than be shown the door the way Portland's coach Mike Dunleavy was after the Lakers swept the Trail Blazers in the first round.

When Mutombo left the game, the sellout crowd of 20,890 showered him with cheers. Was it his last hurrah in a Philadelphia uniform? Mutombo will become a free agent next month. It's uncertain whether he will stay or go his own way like Chris Webber, whom the Lakers likely swept out of Sacramento when they beat the Kings convincingly in the second round.

That's what we mean about the Lakers scorching the landscape. They didn't just beat teams, they rocked them right down to their foundations.

The Lakers rendered Portland coachless and the Kings likely Chrisless. They denuded a San Antonio Spurs team that compiled the best regular-season record and defused league regular-season Most Valuable Player Allen Iverson in these Finals.

"It's amazing how well we've played against the best teams in the league," said Lakers rookie Mark Madsen.

The Lakers have extended a reign that the league's meteorologists had forecast last summer. While confetti falls on the Lakers on Monday during their victory parade, every other team in the league will be bracing for drought conditions.

"I look back to last summer when I was going into predraft workouts," Madsen said, "and every team made references to the Lakers. In Houston, they asked me if I could defend centers, then said, 'We're not asking you to defend Shaquille O'Neal because nobody

can.' In Chicago, they said they were trying to build a championship contender but it was going to be hard as long as Shaquille was a Laker.

"They were almost predicting what has come to pass. I think there is a sense around the NBA of how dominant the Lakers can be."

Can there be any doubters left after the Lakers won 23 of their last 24 games?

To be sure, it took them awhile — roughly six months — to figure out how to play the role of defending NBA champions.

They've now got the script down cold, which is all the more reason for everybody else in the NBA to read this and weep.

"We hadn't won a championship before so we didn't know what that felt like," said Fox, who chipped in 20 points, six rebounds and six assists on Friday. "We didn't know how to handle ourselves. We had to stumble and be embarrassed to really clear up all that mess we created for ourselves."

Don't be surprised if for the foreseeable future the rest of the league looks lost. ∎

Kobe goes up for a dunk in the 3rd quarter of Game 2 of the NBA Finals. He played a terrific all-around game in the series, averaging 24.6 points, 7.8 rebounds, and 5.8 assists per game. (L.A. Daily News: John Lazar)

Kobe Dazzling, Then Dazed

Philly Fans Boo All-Star MVP As He Scores 31 in West Victory

By Billy Witz • February 11, 2002

PHILADELPHIA—Kobe Bryant spent the past few days asking to be loved.

He gushed about his return home, wearing his dad's old Sixers jersey to Friday's media session, eating so many cheese steaks he got sick and promising that, unburdened by the triangle offense, he'd use the NBA All-Star Game as a platform to show off his Philly game.

Then the fans showed theirs. They rolled out their favorite one-word welcome mat: Booooo.

On what should have been a perfect homecoming for Bryant on a night when he scored 31 points, most in an All-Star Game in 14 years, and walked away with the MVP award in the West's 135-120 victory Sunday, the Lakers guard didn't so much feel like a favorite son but a scorned one.

Bryant was booed in pregame introductions by the sellout crowd at First Union Center, but not again until the second half when it became apparent that he was on his way to winning the MVP. When he was given the award at center court, the fans booed so loudly, they drowned out commissioner David Stern.

"I was pretty upset. Pretty hurt," Bryant said, pursing his lips. "I don't know what to say. I can't really describe the feelings that I have when it happened. I'm happy. I'm happy I played well. I'm happy to win the MVP in Philadelphia, and the booing was hurtful, but it's not going to ruin this day for me."

Bryant, who went from Lower Merion High to the Lakers, was booed in his first NBA game here. He solidified his role as a villain last spring when he declared that the Lakers, after splitting the first two games of the NBA Finals in Los Angeles, were coming here to rip the Sixers' hearts out.

Yet, given the festive atmosphere of the weekend, Bryant expected the fans to treat him like a local rather than a Laker.

"I'll use it as motivation, definitely," said Bryant, who won't play here again this season unless it's in the NBA Finals. "I'm the type of person where if something occurs in my life that's hurtful, I'm going to let it hurt me but for so long. I'm going to turn it around and use it as some type of motivation."

Shaquille O'Neal, who was injured and in street clothes, wrapped his arms around Bryant after the award ceremony and whispered in his ear. Everyone else had a word for Bryant, too: Fuhgedaboudit.

These are the same fans, after all, who once booed the son of Phillies Hall of Famer Mike Schmidt at a father-son game and, as the old joke goes, would boo the crack in the Liberty Bell.

"It's a tradition in Philadelphia," former Sixers great

During his fourth All-Star Game appearance Kobe Bryant grabs a rebound in front of the Hornets' Baron Davis. The 2002 NBA All-Star Game marked Kobe's return to his hometown of Philadelphia, where he received a cold reception from fans. (AP Images)

Lakers Join NBA's All-Time Best
2002 NBA Finals: Lakers 113, New Jersey 107

By Howard Beck • June 14, 2002

EAST RUTHERFORD, N.J.—They danced again, sang again, soaked their feet in puddles of sweet champagne again. As if they had never left this scene, this drenched, balmy, comfortably crowded room of half-empty bottles and dripping foreheads and beaming relatives and eternal pride.

The Lakers hollered and they hooted and they puffed out their chests. As if they belonged here. As if they have always lived in this precise moment, straying only for a few months here and there before returning to the glory of it all.

Back to the stage with the glowing trophy. Back to the locker room littered with popped corks and drenched jerseys. Back to the top of the NBA.

It all looked the same. Like a repeat. Like a three-peat. And a sweep-peat. A sweet-peat.

The Lakers entrenched themselves as one of the greatest teams in NBA history Wednesday, completing a four-game Finals sweep of the New Jersey Nets with a 113-107 victory at Continental Airlines Arena.

Three years, three championships, three boisterous celebrations.

If this is all somehow getting to be to routine, no one with the Lakers is complaining.

"It keeps getting better and better every year," said Brian Shaw, his "NBA Champions" hat askew, his black-and-purple leather "Three-peat" jacket still stiff.

The first two championships, over Indiana and Philadelphia, gave the Lakers an identity. The third one put them in elite company.

Only four other teams in league history have won at least three in a row. Only six others have swept a Finals. They became the first Lakers team to sweep the championship round. They won their eighth consecutive Finals game, an NBA record.

"It kind of sets these guys apart as a group," said general manager Mitch Kupchak, ducking out of the locker room.

"Went by fast," Kobe Bryant said of the three-peat. "Unbelievable feeling to have three right now."

It almost seemed anticlimactic, expected, even dull.

"But this one," Derek Fisher said, "is just as special as the first one and the second one."

It ended as it began, with Shaquille O'Neal dominating the game. He finished off the series with 34 points in the finale, then met his stepfather and grandfather in a tearful embrace at midcourt before claiming his third consecutive Finals MVP award. Only Michael Jordan has matched that feat.

It was a fantastic conclusion to a season in which O'Neal fought through injuries to toes and ankles and wrists. But he returned to his dominating self in the Finals and his 145 points were a record for a four-game series. So, incredibly, were his free-throw totals: 68 attempted, 45 made.

"Shaq," said teammate Mitch Richmond, "was a beast." No matter where this goes next, these Lakers will

Kobe Bryant drives around Nets' Jason Kidd in the 2nd quarter of the 2002 NBA Finals. The Lakers dominated the Nets, sweeping them in four games. (L.A. Daily News: John McCoy)

be mentioned among the all-time greatest teams. Amazing, considering the doubts they raised with an uneven, 58-win regular season. More so, considering how close they came to elimination in their seven-game battle with Sacramento in the conference finals.

"It feels great," said Bryant, who had 25 points Wednesday. "This is going to be a hot topic of conversation: Are we one of the best teams ever? And I can live with that. That feels great."

The Lakers claimed the 14th championship in franchise history — their eighth in 22 years — putting them two championships behind the Boston Celtics.

And coach Phil Jackson, who engaged O'Neal in a battle of wills at times and had to force his team to focus in the dullish midseason months, padded his title as the best coach of this era, if not all-time.

The championship was Jackson's ninth as a coach, tying Boston Celtics legend Red Auerbach's record.

"I just look forward to the next one, and great hopes that I have an anticipation of getting back here again for a 10th opportunity," Jackson said. "Looks like I'm going to have to get my own cigar out of my briefcase in the locker room and light it up. I didn't get one FedExed by Red today."

Jackson also earned his 156th postseason victory, moving him past Pat Riley to become the winningest coach in history.

There was more. Shaw and O'Neal became the fourth and fifth players to experience both ends of a Finals sweep. Robert Horry, who won two championships in Houston and now has five, is the first player in Finals history to be on the winning end of sweeps with different franchises.

And so the bottles of Carneros Cuvee and the Domaine Carneros kept popping and spraying and dousing. O'Neal's stepfather, Philip Harrison, sprayed relatives in the hallway outside the locker room.

Minutes earlier, he helped his father, Donald Harrison, down the steps and onto the court. It was an emotional moment for O'Neal, the Newark native who won the title in

Shaquille O'Neal and Kobe Bryant fight for a rebound with several Nets players during Game 2 of the NBA Finals. Shaq won his third straight NBA Finals MVP. (L.A. Daily News: Hans Gutknecht)

front of 80-plus relatives and friends. Soon, his girlfriend, Shaunie Nelson, and their three children, joined the celebration.

"I went to the park where I first started at, last night about 12, 1:30," O'Neal said. "As a youngster, I used to play with the raggedy basketball my father got me. I just used to dream about certain things. I just stuck with it and all my dreams have come true."

All around, it was a family celebration. Rick Fox, with his daughter and his father. Derek Fisher, doing interviews flanked by his brother, Duane Washington, and his parents, Annette and John Fisher.

Jackson was met on the court by his five sons and daughters.

There was something in this championship for everyone. Richmond, a six-time All-Star who sacrificed minutes and money, won his first title. So did Samaki Walker, who turned down more money last summer, and Lindsey Hunter. Devean George, who finished the Finals with a strong performance, got his third ring in three pro seasons, and another reason to consider re-signing with the Lakers this summer.

The three-peat did not finally come into focus until the final minutes.

Fisher and O'Neal combined for a 3-point play. Bryant hit a runner in the lane. O'Neal made a pair of free throws. Bryant hit a driving layup.

The Nets called timeout with 3:32 left, the Lakers up 104-95, and Bryant skipped toward the bench, meeting Mark Madsen in a flying chest bump. George started shaking his left hand downward, the last three fingers sticking out.

Across the court, Snoop Dogg danced in front of his courtside seat and waved a Lakers towel.

"This is awesome, this is too much," Fox said. "How many more? You want a prediction? I know at least two more. I see that." ∎

Kobe, joined by his wife Vanessa, gives the cheering crowd a three-peat sign during the Lakers 2002 championship victory parade along Figueroa street. (Press-Telegram: Steven Georges)

Bryant's History Score: 81

Point Total Is Second-Most Ever in NBA — Oh, and Lakers Also Rally for Win

By Ross Siler • January 23, 2006

When it was thrown around in the aftermath of Kobe Bryant's 62-point game in three quarters against the Dallas Mavericks, the number seemed like nothing more than a footnote to one of the greatest nights in the superstar guard's career.

Nobody ever had scored 80 points in an NBA game except for Wilt Chamberlain on one immortal night in Hershey, Pa., and nobody would ever again. Until Bryant, only 33 days after the Dallas game, did the unthinkable Sunday night at Staples Center.

The box score doesn't look believable unless you were there. Bryant finished with 81 points, 55 in the second half, single-handedly bringing the Lakers back from 18 points down in the third quarter in a 122-104 victory over the Toronto Raptors.

"It hasn't really sank in yet," Bryant said. "We have four days off coming up here and I would have been sick as a dog if we'd lost this game. I just wanted to step up and inspire them to play a better game and it turned into something pretty special."

"To sit here and say that I grasp what happened tonight, I'd be lying," Bryant later added.

The short list of players to score even 70 in an NBA game includes only Chamberlain, David Thompson, Elgin Baylor and David Robinson. Bryant sank seven free throws in the last 2 1/2 minutes to write his name second to Chamberlain in the record books.

There were no cameras to record Chamberlain's 100-point game on March 2, 1962, while Bryant's night was broadcast live in two countries. He was asked in a packed interview room afterward if he ever could have fathomed scoring 80 points.

"Not even in my dreams," Bryant said. "It's something that just kind of happened. It's tough to explain. I don't know, it's just one of those things."

Bryant departed to roars with 4.2 seconds left and public address announcer Lawrence Tanter advising fans to save their ticket stubs. On his way to the bench, Bryant shared a hug with Lakers coach Phil Jackson, the significance of which was not lost on Bryant.

"It's special because we've been through so much," said Bryant, who was called uncoachable by Jackson in the coach's best-selling diary of the 2003-04 season. "We've been through so many battles, we've been through so many things.

"And it's special for me because when I play the game, I play the game to try to please him. If he's happy with my performance, it makes me happy because I learned the game from him. ... He just looked at me and

Kobe Bryant dunks for two of his career high 81-point against the Raptors. Kobe's 81 points are second all-time in the NBA in a single game, only behind Wilt Chamberlain's 100 in 1962. (Daily Breeze: Scott Varley)

smiled at me and said he was proud of the way I played."

Jackson, who sat Bryant for six minutes at the start of the second quarter, with the Lakers falling behind by 14 in the process, relayed an exchange he had late in the fourth quarter with assistant coach Frank Hamblen on the bench.

Needless to say, Jackson wasn't keeping track of how many points Bryant had totaled on the night.

"I said, 'I think I'd better take him out now, I think this is a time where I felt the game was sealed,'" Jackson said. "He said, 'I don't think you can. He's got 77 points.' So we stayed with it until he hit 80."

Bryant went 28 of 46, 7 of 13 from 3-point range and 18 of 20 from the foul line. He had 14 points in the first quarter, 12 in the second, 27 in the third and 28 in the fourth. The Raptors tried everyone from Morris Peterson to Jose Calderon in an attempt to stop him.

The only blemish on the night? Bryant's franchise-record streak of consecutive made free throws came to an end at 62 in the final minute of the first half.

"To be honest with you, that's not exactly the way you want to have a team win a game," Jackson said of the one-man show. "But when you have to win a game, it's great to be able to have that weapon to do it with."

Rookie center Andrew Bynum, an Xbox player, summed up Bryant's night by saying, "He's the human joystick of basketball."

Center Chris Mihm was asked about the 100-point game and pointed out that the 7-foot-1 Chamberlain probably got most of his points around the basket. Bryant got 81 on jump shots and drives and went to the foul line only once in the third quarter.

As hard as it might be to believe, the game could have gone the other way in the second half. The Lakers trailed 69-51 as Matt Bonner hit a 3-pointer with 9:55 left in the third, staring at a loss to one of the NBA's lowliest teams.

"We're a team that comes out flat in the third quarter," guard Smush Parker said, "and it could have definitely got ugly and we could have just gave up."

But Bryant connected on four 3-pointers, scoring 27 of the Lakers' 42 points in the third. He capped the quarter by jumping to get a hand on a Mike James pass in the backcourt, beating Calderon to the ball and throwing down a two-handed dunk to put the Lakers in front 87-85.

With the Lakers leading 91-85, Bryant finally got his chance to play in the fourth quarter, something that didn't happen in the Dallas game. Bryant hit 7 of 13 shots in the fourth and 12 of 13 free throws, the crowd on its feet for almost every one.

"When he had like 57 and there were 11 minutes left in the game," Mihm said, "we were like, 'Oh, boy.' I said 72. Obviously, I was quite shy."

On a historic night, Bryant said the most memorable thing might have been a phone call he took in the locker room from Magic Johnson afterward.

"That meant more to me than the game itself because I idolized him as a kid," Bryant said, "and for him to call me and tell me what a great game it was and how proud of me he is, that meant more to me than 81 points."

The Lakers reached the midpoint of their season at 22-19 with the victory. The only question left is what Bryant, now averaging an astounding 35.9 points per game, will do for an encore. ∎

Kobe gets a hug from his coach Phil Jackson and cheers from his teammates as he exits his historic 81-point performance. (Daily Breeze: Scott Varley)

LA is the City of Stars ... and MVPs

Kobe Adds to L.A.'s Status as the MVP Capital of America

By Stephen Dilbeck • May 6, 2008

We have the stars, baby.

The glitz, the glamour, the Hollywood sign, the premiers, Jack sitting courtside, and one other little thing — most sports MVPs in the country.

No city has captured more of the top professional awards in the four major sports than Los Angeles. We are just so cool.

Compared to L.A., New York is the city that sleeps. Chicago is a second city. Boston the cradle of almost. Philadelphia the city of brotherly runner-ups.

That's right, Kobe Bryant's MVP award today only will increase Los Angeles' lead as the sporting MVP capital of all America.

This comes with a semi-convenient qualifier, heavy on the semi.

We're talking most individual MVPs since the 1960-61 seasons, when the Lakers headed west and the Angels opened shop. We're talking the most different individuals to win the award.

Bryant's MVP will give the Los Angeles area, including Anaheim, a lucky total of 13.

That gives Los Angeles two more athletes to win an MVP than New York and Boston.

One more if Boston tried to count Joe Thorton, who played just 23 games with the Bruins in the 2005-06 season before skating 58 games with the Sharks and really capturing the Hart Memorial Trophy in San Jose.

It's Los Angeles claiming one more little piece of sports significance, if a particularly showy one. Turn on the searchlights, wrap the whole city in Wayfarers.

The stars really are here.

L.A.'s MVPs aren't sports figures who burned brightly for a season and then disappeared, either.

These are the megastars of stars. Koufax, Magic, Gretzky, Kareem, Gibson, Shaq. Guys you can identify by one name.

And now Kobe. Simply the best basketball player on the planet. Not to mention Pluto.

The spotlight found these guys wherever they were. Players who had impact beyond local borders. National figures, players in or headed for a hall of fame.

Names mentioned in any "greatest ever" conversations.

Los Angeles has managed to lead this MVP tally despite not having an NFL team for the past 14 seasons. That's like L.A. winning a race of four-cylinders, down one piston.

Baseball has led the MVP way in Los Angeles, with the Dodgers and Angels combining to have six players named MVP.

During Kobe's 2008 NBA MVP season he averaged 28.3 points, 6.3 rebounds, and 5.4 assists per game. (L.A. Daily News: Hans Gutknecht)

Of course, baseball offers two MVPs every year, one for each league. Only one is awarded in the NBA, the NFL and NHL.

Los Angeles also has two hockey teams — the Ducks were unsuccessful in nabbing an MVP honor during last season's Stanley Cup run — and two NBA teams. Somehow the Clippers have failed to add to the L.A. total. Try to recover from the shock.

The Dodgers gave Los Angeles its first MVP back in 1962 when shortstop Maury Wills almost single-handedly changed baseball when he stole a record 104 bases.

The next season, Sandy Koufax, the most dominating left-hander in baseball history, made it consecutive MVPs for the Dodgers.

Steve Garvey added one more in 1974, and Kirk Gibson yet another in 1988, which just happens to be the last time the Dodgers actually won a playoff series.

The Angels got into the act in 1979, when Don Baylor drove in 139 runs and led them to their first playoff appearance. Vladimir Guerrero gave the Angels their second MVP in 2004.

That means a lot of famous Dodgers — Don Drysdale, Tommy Davis, Fernando Valenzuela, Mike Piazza — and Angels — Jim Fregosi, Nolan Ryan, Bobby Grich, Troy Glaus — have never been honored.

Bryant's award will leave the Lakers tied with the Dodgers for most MVPs in L.A. Kareem Abdul-Jabbar (a winner three times as a Laker, six overall), Magic Johnson (also three) and Shaquille O'Neal all preceded Bryant.

It never happened for Jerry West or Elgin Baylor. The Rams gave us Roman Gabriel, back when he

was still talking to his son, and the Raiders' Marcus Allen, back when he was still talking to Al Davis. The Kings gave us Gretzky.

We consider Anaheim part of Los Angeles — just ask Arte Moreno does — but Oakland a separate animal from San Francisco. (If those two were combined, they would have 17 MVPs; the A's with a staggering seven and the Giants — who have never won a World Series — with five).

The NFL's MVP is voted upon by members of the Associated Press. In the MLB and NHL it's awarded by beat writers, the NBA by beat writers and broadcasters.

It's makes for prestigious stuff, a city of stars that also officially is the leading producer of the best professional athletes for more than 40 years.

Sure, things are different here. There's a lot of preening going on down Staples Center aisles. Way too much effort into the look. Luxury boxes at all arenas and stadiums are jammed with the affluent.

But since 1961, no city has been treated to a more gifted and successful group of sports superstars.

In L.A., the stars always seem out. ■

Kobe Bryant holds up the MVP trophy before Game 2 of the Western Conference Semi-Finals vs. the Utah Jazz. Bryant won the award over Chris Paul and Kevin Garnett. (San Gabriel Valley Tribune: Keith Birmingham)

USA's Kobe Bryant finishes the dunk emphatically vs. Australia during the Beijing 2008 Olympics. Team USA beat Australia 116-85 in the quarterfinals. (AP Images)

2008 OLYMPICS

USA's Kobe Bryant goes up for a dunk against Spain during a men's preliminary game at the Beijing 2008 Olympics. (AP Images)

Team USA's Kobe Bryant bites his gold medal during ceremonies following their win over Spain in the Gold Medal Game at the Beijing 2008 Olympics. Kobe scored 20 points in the game, including several clutch shots down the stretch to clinch the 118-107 victory. (AP Images)

USA's Kobe Bryant sticks out his tongue as he gets set during the men's Gold Medal Game against Spain at the Beijing 2008 Olympics. Kobe bested his Lakers teammate and good friend Pau Gasol in the final game. (AP Images)

X-cellent

Lakers Beat Orlando for Their 10th Championship in Los Angeles, as Coach Phil Jackson Surpasses Red Auerbach with 10th NBA Title

By Elliott Teaford • June 15, 2009

ORLANDO—Redemption day finally arrived for the Lakers.

If they shed tears on a hot and humid Sunday night, they were tears of joy instead of tears of anguish. They exorcised their demons with a victory dance after their 99-86 victory over the Orlando Magic in the decisive Game 5 of the NBA Finals.

The Lakers locked arms and bounced up and down after the final buzzer sounded on their 4-1 series victory over the Magic at Amway Arena. Thousands of Lakers fans, who had appeared as if from nowhere for Game 5, bellowed louder from the stands.

Three days shy of the one-year anniversary of a humiliating 39-point loss to the Boston Celtics in the decisive Game 6 last June, the Lakers gleefully celebrated the 15th championship in franchise history. Only the Celtics, with 17 titles, have won more.

"I can't believe this moment is here," Kobe Bryant said after he had 30 points, six rebounds, five assists and four blocks in a little more than 43 minutes in Game 5.

For Bryant and the Lakers, the journey to their championship began with a renewed commitment to defense. The Celtics torched them in last year's Finals. The Lakers also had to get tougher after Boston pushed them around.

Getting back to the Finals, and winning, was the team's lone goal for 2008-09.

Bryant revealed several times during the playoffs that he was too preoccupied with chasing the title to sleep and said he occasionally swapped text messages with Pau Gasol at 3 a.m., which meant Gasol also was awake at that hour.

"Having gone through what we went through last year and having the goal in mind of trying to get back to this point, and to have the attitude of (trying) to become a better defensive team, a better rebounding team, and then to actually do it and to see it all happen, it feels like I'm dreaming right now," Bryant said.

This was Phil Jackson's 10th NBA title as a coach, breaking his tie with the late Red Auerbach, and Bryant's fourth. Bryant won his first three with Shaquille O'Neal in an almost unbeatable inside-outside combination.

This time, he did it without O'Neal.

"Well, I don't have to hear that criticism, that idiotic

Kobe enters the court during player introductions of Game 1 of the 2009 NBA Finals vs. the Orlando Magic, at Staples Center. (L.A. Daily News: Sean Hiller)

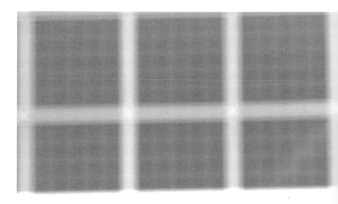

"criticism anymore," a laughing Bryant said of winning a championship without O'Neal. "That's the biggest thing. I don't have to hear that stuff anymore."

Bryant was selected the winner of the Bill Russell Award as the Most Valuable Player of the Finals. He averaged 32.4 points, 5.6 rebounds and 7.4 assists in five games and earned the honor for the first time in six trips to the championship round.

O'Neal was named the Finals MVP in each of the Lakers' victories earlier this decade. He was traded to the Miami Heat after the Lakers' loss to Detroit, when management revamped the roster in dramatic fashion in the summer of 2004.

"Congratulations, Kobe, you deserve it," O'Neal wrote on his Twitter feed immediately after the game. "You played great. Enjoy it, my man, enjoy it."

The Lakers' six Finals appearances this decade matched the number the Jackson-coached and Michael Jordan-led Chicago Bulls made in the 1990s. The difference was the Bulls went 6-for-6 during their remarkable run.

The Lakers' victory also broke a tie with the San Antonio Spurs for the most titles in this decade. The Spurs won championships in 2003 over New Jersey, in 2005 over the Pistons and in 2007 over Cleveland, while Orlando lost for the second time in as many Finals. Houston swept O'Neal and the Magic in 1995. O'Neal left the Magic the following season as a free agent and joined forces with Bryant.

Jackson arrived to coach them in 1999.

It was Trevor Ariza, rather than Bryant, who helped the Lakers break open Game 5. Ariza, a former member of the Magic, scored 11 of his 15 points in the second quarter. He ignited an 18-2 run that propelled the Lakers to a 56-46 halftime lead.

The Lakers turned up their defensive pressure in the third quarter, held the Magic to only 15 points and then

Kobe Bryant waves to fans as he rides a bus with his daughters, passing by Staples Center en route to the Los Angeles Memorial Coliseum during the Lakers' 2009 championship parade. (L.A. Daily News: Hans Gutknecht)

coasted home with a workmanlike effort in the fourth. Their lead ballooned to as many as 18 points in the final period.

"Well, it's a dream, a dream come true," said Gasol, who had 14 points, a team-leading 15 rebounds and a whole new collection of bruises from trying to contain Orlando's Dwight Howard (11 points and 10 rebounds).

Lamar Odom had 17 points and 10 rebounds for the Lakers, and Derek Fisher had 13 points while joining with Bryant to win his fourth title.

"We set a goal early in training camp and that was to win the NBA championship," Odom said after winning his first title. "Every time we came in as a group, we left that group by saying, '1, 2, 3, ring.' We set a goal and we attained it." ■

Above: Kobe attacks the basket as the Orlando Magic's Marcin Gortat defends during Game 1 of the NBA Finals. He finished with 40 points in the game, en route to his first NBA Finals MVP. (L.A. Daily News: Hans Gutknecht) Opposite: Kobe and the Lakers received their 2009 Championship rings before they opened the 2009-2010 season against the Clippers. For the fourth time in his career, Kobe gets a ring from NBA commissioner David Stern. (L.A. Daily News: Sean Hiller)

An Ugly Game, But Beautiful Finish

Kobe Wins 5th Title and 2nd Finals MVP

By Vincent Bonsignore • June 18, 2010

It was ugly, repulsive, as hideous a basketball game as you've ever seen.

But it was oh, so beautiful at the same time.

It was like suffering through 80 minutes of the worst movie of all time, only to have the final 10 minutes grab you like you've never been grabbed before, then rushing out of the theater feeling on top of the world.

It was Kobe Bryant at his very worst, a tired, laboring, uncertain shell of himself through the biggest game of his life. Bryant missed 18 of his 24 shots and 5 of 11 of his free throws; he had four turnovers and a handful of other tentative plays that resulted in empty possessions.

Yet he was at his best when it counted most, mustering everything he had to help carry the Lakers over the Boston Celtics in a tense, anxious, restless fourth quarter, scoring 10 of his 23 points down the stretch and grabbing every rebound as the Lakers overcame their hated nemesis 83-79 in Game 7 of the NBA Finals Thursday at Staples Center.

The difference?

Bryant sitting down to start the fourth quarter, a decision by Phil Jackson to settle his superstar down.

"He was a little too animated, trying too hard," Jackson said. "He's a guy who can try hard and get things done by sheer will. This wasn't one of those nights."

But by the time Bryant returned, he was ready to help carry the Lakers.

"He came back and gave us the help we needed down the stretch," Jackson said. "He found himself frustrated out there for a number of minutes. Little things, like the ball coming out of his hands. Not being able to complete plays, things like that.

"But he stayed with it and helped his team with the game."

Bryant was named the MVP of the series; an honor achieved more for the body of his work in this series than what he did Thursday. But when he raised his MVP trophy afterward in front of an adoring crowd, he did so proudly and triumphantly.

And in doing so, he finally acknowledged what everyone knew to be true, but something he was so reluctant to admit through this splendid final.

Bryant fully understood the history between the Lakers and the Celtics, and he respected it and embraced it.

He pretended to ignore the implications of this great rivalry over the course of the series, never once

Kobe Bryant celebrates after winning Game 7 of the NBA Finals at the Staples Center vs. the Celtics. The Lakers beat the Celtics 83-79 to win their second consecutive NBA Championship and Kobe's second consecutive NBA Finals MVP. (L.A. Daily News: Hans Gutknecht)

showing a hint of awareness for the rivalry or an ounce
of passion over the possibility of beating the Celtics while
wearing a Lakers uniform.

But deep down inside, he understood it, was aware of
it and wanted a victory over Boston in the worst way. And
when he got it, when the championship was finally his and
as he clutched his championship trophy at midcourt of
Staples Center, he acknowledged the obvious.

This was the most memorable of the five championships
he's won with the Lakers over the years, offering a tip of
the cap to the Celtics and the clear place they hold deep in
the soul of every Lakers fan and every player that has ever
donned the purple and gold.

"This is the sweetest," Bryant said.

Everything else, the lack of recognition for the rivalry
or the stakes or the Lakers' disappointing history over the
Celtics, who had beaten them in the Finals nine times in 11
meetings over the years and all four times the series went
the distance, was just posturing.

"I was just lying to you guys," he said "You guys know
what kind of basketball historian I am. I know ever series
the Lakers have every played in, every Celtic series, every
statistic. But I had to focus on the series.

"We had to downplay the rivalry through the course of
the series so we could focus on what we had to do."

But he didn't do it alone, not by a long shot.

Ron Artest, so often looking out of sorts in the triangle
offense in his first year with the Lakers, finished with 20
points and five steals while doing his usual defensive job on
Paul Pierce.

"Ron was the MVP of the game," Jackson said.

Pau Gasol agreed. "I'm so happy for Ron the way he
played this game," Gasol said. "He was very productive and
confident and aggressive. He was a huge part of our success."

So was Gasol, who has listened for two years about how
he was too soft to stand up to a tough, physical team like the
Celtics after the Lakers fell to Boston in the 2008 Finals.

Confetti falls as Kobe Bryant celebrates on top of the scorers
table after wining the championship. He averaged 28.6 points
and 8 rebounds on his way to the MVP award. (L.A. Daily News:
John McCoy)

Gasol finished with 19 points and 18 rebounds Thursday, dispelling forever any talk of him being too soft.

The 7-foot Spaniard has been with the Lakers 2 1/2 seasons now — getting rescued from the Memphis Grizzlies in one of the all-time great steal trades of all time — and gone to three NBA Finals, winning two of them.

And he realizes what a charmed life he's leading in the NBA.

"For me it's incredible," Gasol said "It's like I'm living in a different dimension, right? If I had a genie and asked for a wish this would be my wish for my life and my basketball career."

Together, Gasol and the rest of the Lakers carried Bryant, keeping the game close enough to give their superstar teammate a chance to help win it down the stretch.

For Bryant, it was a position he's never been in — wanting something so much he almost tried too hard to get it.

"I just wanted it so bad. So So bad and on top of that I was beat," Bryant said. "I was really really tired and the more I tried to push the more it got away from me. I'm so thankful for my teammates keeping it close.

"My guys picked me up, big time."

And so did Staples Center, which was as loud and crazy as it's ever been.

"I can't say enough about these fans," Bryant said.

They lifted him, lifted the Lakers, who rewarded them with the 16th championship in franchise history.

It wasn't pretty, but it sure was beautiful. ∎

Right: Kobe shoots as Boston Celtics' Ray Allen defends during Game 7 of the NBA Finals. (L.A. Daily News: Hans Gutknecht) Opposite: The "Black Mamba" Kobe Bryant smiles as he holds the championship trophy during the celebration of his fifth NBA championship. (L.A. Daily News: Hans Gutknecht)

USA's Kobe Bryant jumps for the layup as teammate Kevin Love looks on during the men's Gold Medal Game at the London 2012 Olympics. (AP Images)

2012 OLYMPICS

Kobe kisses his Gold Medal, the second in his Olympic collection. He averaged 12.1 points in the tournament. (AP Images)

Kevin Durant, Carmelo Anthony, LeBron James and Kobe Bryant celebrate their Gold Medal victory at the London 2012 Olympics. (AP Images)

Kobe looks backward as he lines up a reverse dunk in a 156-73 win over Nigeria at the London 2012 Olympics. He finished with 16 points in the game. (AP Images)

Respect

Lakers' Kobe Bryant Considers Memphis' Tony Allen Best Defender

By Mark Medina • November 26, 2014

The phone call appeared pretty routine. At least it seemed normal enough that the conversation involved just two former teammates catching up.

But then Memphis forward Tony Allen asked Lakers forward Ed Davis something that had stayed on his mind for basically his entire 10-year NBA career.

"How does Kobe Bryant look?" Allen asked Davis early in training camp, aware that the Lakers' star 36-year-old guard had played just six games last season because of injuries to his left Achilles tendon and left knee.

Davis spent the previous two seasons with the Grizzlies aware that Allen "lives for playing against Kobe." That explains why Davis viewed Allen's question as a devious attempt to obtain what Davis called "inside information." Perhaps it could become useful for when Allen defends Bryant, including when the Lakers (3-11) host the Memphis Grizzlies (12-2) on Wednesday at Staples Center. After all, Bryant averages a league-leading 26.7 points albeit on only 38.1 percent shooting.

So, Davis refused to answer Allen's question. Davis then exposed his undercover tactics to a reporter, something that left Allen laughing when confronted about the incident.

"I just asked him how Kobe looked," Allen said in an interview with Los Angeles News Group. "That's all I asked. He didn't give me too much anyway, so it was a dead question."

Still, Bryant raised his eyebrows when he learned about Allen's attempt at gaining an edge in a matchup that evokes memories of him watching former Lakers forward Michael Cooper defend Boston Celtics forward Larry Bird during the "Showtime Era."

"That's the classic art of war. We always have to get some (advantage) any chance you can." Bryant told the Los Angeles News Group. "Tony knows I'm pretty straight forward. He knows I'm going to try to post him, get to my spots and abuse him. And he's going to fight me like a dog to keep me off my spots."

This tactic also explains the thought process between two competitors who believe they both excel and struggle the most when they play against each other.

Memorable Battles

Bryant waxed nostalgic about seeing Cooper guard Bird through three NBA Finals (1984, 1985, 1987). Bryant loved how neither player backed down from the physically bruising play that defined the NBA in the '80s. It's not a stretch to see some similarities in the Bryant-Allen matchup.

Cooper won the 1987 NBA Defensive Player of the Year award and was named to the league's all-defensive first team five times. Allen earned all-defensive first-team honors twice and joined the second team once.

Kobe Bryant goes to the hoop as Boston Celtics guard Tony Allen defends during Game 6 of the 2010 NBA Finals. The Lakers beat the Celtics 89-67 to force Game 7. (L.A. Daily News: Hans Gutknecht)

Bird is considered among the NBA's best 3-point shooter, while Bryant ranks fourth on the NBA's all-time scoring list. Cooper's Lakers had a 2-1 NBA Finals edge over Bird's Celtics, while Bryant and Allen are squared up 1-1 in Lakers-Celtics Finals matchups (2008, 2010).

"He earned the right to be who he is. I'm basically trying to hold my case as being one of the best defenders in the game," Allen said. "I've been in the league 10 years trying to study (Kobe). But he comes with something new all the time. That's what makes the competition fun."

The competition has played out in various ways.

Allen sat out the first three games of the 2008 NBA Finals and then played only 19 minutes for the next three games that ended with a Celtics championship. But in Game 2 of the 2010 NBA Finals, Allen held Bryant to a 5-of-14 second-half clip and forced seven turnovers. But that hardly stopped the Lakers from winning in seven games.

Allen lasted only eight minutes before fouling out in his rookie debut on Feb. 22, 2005. But then two years later, on Dec. 2007, Allen held Bryant to 22 points on a 6-of-25 clip in a Lakers' 110-91 loss.

Yet, Allen hardly gloats about his success.

"I don't feel anything," Allen said. "Kobe's confidence level is as high as anybody's. If he misses, he feels he can shoot it again and will make it."

Bryant sure can. He has strung together two 40-point games and two 30-point games against Allen in stints with Boston (2004-2010) and Memphis (2010-present).

"I know what to do and he knows how to guard me," Bryant said. "It's just a matter of who can get the better of who consistently. There will be possessions where he does a phenomenal job. There will be possessions where I abuse him. It's a fun battle to see."

And it's one that Lakers coach Byron Scott describes as a game of "cat and mouse." Both Scott and Grizzlies coach Dave Joerger observe Allen repeatedly tries to play physical with Bryant to deny him both the ball and open shots. But both coaches notice Bryant responds both by playing through the contact and compensating with his footwork, pump fakes and off-ball cuts.

"I want them to play against each other for the next 12 years," Joerger said. "It's awesome competition and it's a great thing to be a part of and watch."

Mutual Respect

Bryant displays his love for the NBA's history and current-day storylines in various ways. He talks endlessly about studying past NBA greats. Bryant will share how he has mentored a slew of current NBA stars. He will gladly discuss up-and-coming players, offering both positive reinforcement and constructive criticism.

Yet, Bryant hardly has shown much enthusiasm for praising a defender, particularly when that player may have contributed to a poor shooting night. When it comes to talking about Allen, though, that becomes a different story.

"He's fundamentally sound defensively and he plays harder than everybody else defensively," Bryant said. "He has a competitive desire to compete individually. That's very uncommon. Most defensive players I face want help all the time. I've never heard him ask for help. He likes taking the challenge."

Kobe and Tony Allen had many battles over the years, most notably in the 2010 NBA Finals. (L.A. Daily News: Hans Gutknecht)

So much that Allen hardly seems interested in adopting a typical defender's mentality by undercutting his opponent either through the press or on the court.

"There's no talking in the battle," Allen said. "There's no use for talking. I use everything that I prepare for in the offseason and in practice and the team scheme."

That mutual respect reached unforeseen heights during the Lakers' 96-92 win on Dec. 17, 2013 in Memphis.

Bryant reported feeling encouraged that he scored 21 points on 9-of-18 shooting against Allen in only his sixth game since returning from a left Achilles injury that had kept him sidelined for eight months.

"I felt like during that game if I could get to spots on the floor against Tony, I could do it against anybody," Bryant said. "During that game, I felt really good about it with the limitations I had and how to work my way through them."

Allen walked away impressed with Bryant's performance. But Allen also walked away devastated that their knee collision early in the second half resulted in Bryant suffering a left knee injury that would sideline him for the season.

Amid fans accusing Allen on Twitter of causing the injury, he quickly reached out and apologized to Bryant. But knowing Bryant played against him for nearly an entire half on one healthy leg, Allen sat by his locker stall less than a year later still struggling to process it all.

"He does everything. There's nothing he can't do," Allen said of Bryant. "It just shows you he's a tough-minded guy. You have to respect that." ■

Bryant and Allen have a mutual respect for how tenaciously they each play the game. (L.A. Daily News: David Crane)

Who's Better?

Kobe on Verge of Surpassing Michael Jordan on NBA's All-Time Scoring List

By Mark Medina • December 11, 2014

Kobe Bryant sat on the team bus, offering unmatched confidence as a high school senior on how he would fare against one of his favorite idols.

"I remember Kobe saying, 'Michael Jordan can't stop me,'" said David Lasman, one of Bryant's former teammates at Lower Merion, a suburban high school outside Philadelphia. "'I'm not saying I can stop him. But he can't stop me.'"

Lasman would tell the 17-year-old Bryant he's "crazy" for saying something so brash. After all, Jordan would win six NBA championships, six Finals MVPs and five regular-season MVPS. But Bryant would eventually enter the NBA out of high school, win five NBA championships with the Lakers and spark never-ending comparisons to Jordan.

Bryant could also surpass Jordan for third place on the NBA's all-time scoring list when the Lakers (6-16) visit San Antonio (15-6) on Friday at AT&T Center. Bryant only needs 31 points to surpass Jordan's 32,292 career points. Bryant conceded his upcoming milestone will mark "a great accomplishment," trailing only Karl Malone (36,928) and former Lakers legend Kareem Abdul-Jabbar (38,387) on the scoring list. But Bryant argued "the true beauty in it comes in the journey."

That journey took Bryant down plenty of winding roads and intersections that involved Jordan.

The Beginning

It all started once Bryant announced in 1996 he would jump from high school to the NBA. Once the Lakers secured his rights for the 13th pick, that move enabled Bryant to play against Jordan before retiring.

"That was a big factor," said Gregg Downer, Bryant's high school coach at Lower Merion. "I don't think Kobe had any real desire to go to college. He wanted to test his skills right away against the very best."

After all, Bryant said he spent his childhood studying tape of "absolutely everybody."

Bryant then ticked off a list of NBA's greats, including former Lakers (Magic Johnson, Jerry West, James Worthy, George Mikan), other guards (Oscar Robertson, Walt Frazier) and even big men (Bill Russell, Bob Petit). Bryant credited his strong fundamentals and scoring abilities to those players, including Jordan.

"He talked about that he wanted to be the best player in the NBA," said Lakers coach Byron Scott, who mentored Bryant his rookie season. "I told him, 'You would be.' I know how hard he worked."

Yet, Bryant maintained his focus, which had more to do with expediting his development than worrying about individual accolades.

"If I really paid attention to numbers and was hell bent on passing records, I would've gone to college,"

Kobe backs down the legendary Michael Jordan during a February, 1998 match-up with the Bulls. (San Gabriel Valley Tribune: Keith Birmingham)

Bryant said. "I came to the pros and was ready to play. I put up big numbers there, but I sat on the bench for my first three years in the league."

The Interactions

The comparisons to Jordan soon became inescapable, including their scoring mentality, on-court mannerisms, interviews and lucrative endorsement deals. Bryant disliked that narrative out of respect for Jordan's resume. But Bryant said he spent less time consumed with that hype and more occupied with learning how to be like Mike.

"When I first came into the league, Michael was terrifying everybody," Bryant said. "I was willing to challenge and learn from him. I wasn't afraid to call him and ask him questions. He was open and spoke to me a lot and helped me a lot."

Bryant would not divulge what those lessons entailed, other than talking about various unspecified "post moves." But it did not take long for those talks to morph into competitive matchups.

The 1998 NBA All-Star Game featured Jordan and Bryant together, creating the inevitable storyline between the two players. Jordan posted 23 points on 10-of-18 shooting in the East's 135-114 victory and won his third of All-Star MVP. Though he didn't even start for the Lakers, the 19-year-old Bryant started for the West and finished with 18 points on 7-of-16 shooting, six rebounds and two steals despite missing the entire fourth quarter.

"I was accused of taking Kobe out of the game because I wanted Michael to win MVP," said George Karl, who coached the 1998 Western Conference All-Star team and currently serves as an ESPN analyst. "I never in my life would think of something like that. At an all-star

Right: When Michael Jordan returned to the NBA with the Washington Wizards, Kobe had taken his place as one of the dominant presences and superstars of the league. (AP Images) Opposite: Michael Jordan goes up for a layup and Shaquille O'Neal challenges the shot as a young Kobe Bryant looks on. (San Gabriel Valley Tribune: Keith Birmingham)

game, you're just trying to manage everybody's minutes."

Six years later, there was no debate on which player won in their last matchup.

In what marked his final season of his 15-year career and his second comeback attempt, the 40-year-old Jordan hardly received a farewell pleasantry when the Lakers hosted the Washington Wizards on March 23, 2003. While Jordan ended with 23 points on 10-of-20 shooting in 41 minutes, Bryant dropped 55 points on a 15-of-29 clip. Bryant's points came from everywhere, including from 3-point range (9 of 13) and from the foul line (16 of 18).

"The basketball historians will look back on that and probably talk about the passing of the torch," said Lakers assistant coach Mark Madsen, who played with Bryant that season. "But in my mind it was just a masterful performance and an important game for us. The one thing about Kobe is he's never been afraid of any moment."

The Comparisons

Their ability to thrive through any moment explains why the Bryant-Jordan comparisons never fade.

Bryant has scored a career-high 81 points. He has posted at least 50 points in 24 games. Bryant's career-high 35.4 points-per-game average in the 2005-06 season represented the eighth-highest scoring average in league history. Meanwhile, Jordan has scored a career-high 69 points. He posted at least 50 points in 39 games. Jordan's 30.1 points-per-game career average eclipsed Bryant's average in all but two of his seasons.

That prompted former Lakers and Bulls coach Phil Jackson to offer his analysis of the two players he coached in his recent memoir, "Eleven Rings." Jackson considered Jordan a better defender, more accurate shooter and superior leader, while praising Bryant's conditioning and offseason training. Jackson also wrote Bryant seemed "hell bent on surpassing Jordan as the greatest player in the game."

"People who say that don't really understand me," Bryant said. "It's a myth. Phil likes to say things a lot of times to create good content and good stories."

Kobe and MJ shared many similar traits on the court and similarly blossomed under the tutelage of coach Phil Jackson. (L.A. Daily News: Hans Gutknecht)

More stories will surface once Bryant surpasses Jordan on the scoring list. If it happens against San Antonio, Bryant would have needed to play 196 more games than Jordan. Yet, consider some circumstances. While Jordan remained the undisputed leader of his team, Bryant played behind Shaquille O'Neal before eventually becoming the Lakers' first option. Bryant also played 19 consecutive seasons, while Jordan rested between two separate comebacks.

Both Bryant and Jordan also relied on their fundamentals late in their careers to offset lost athleticism. Bryant has averaged a league-leading 25.5 points albeit on a career-low 39 percent shooting after playing in only six games last season with injuries to his left Achilles tendon and left knee. In his last two seasons with the Wizards, Jordan averaged between 20 and 23 points per game.

But Bryant solely remains worried Jordan's six NBA titles.

"When I grew up looking at Magic, Russell and Michael, it's all measured about that," Bryant said. "It wasn't about one championship or two. It was you had to win five or six."

And unlike his brash talking as a 17-year-old senior, Bryant did not share this standard with teammates.

"Kobe never spoke of trying to surpass this guy or that guy. He just worked every day," said Nuggets coach Brian Shaw, Bryant's former teammate and assistant coach. "It's not an accident he's as good as he is. It didn't just happen. He put in the time."

Now that he has, Bryant believes he has achieved something besides adding fuel to the comparisons with Jordan. Bryant carved his own identity.

"We've had different career paths," Bryant said. "But I feel a great sense of accomplishment having to carry on the two-guard legacy from Jerry to Michael to myself." ∎

Right: Chicago Bulls' Michael Jordan reaches to defend Kobe's jumper. (AP Images) Opposite: Kobe was often compared to Jordan and measured by his accomplishments throughout his career but emerged as an NBA superstar and icon unlike any before or after. (AP Images)

Inspiration, Competition, Admiration

How Kobe Bryant's Relationship with LeBron James Evolved

By Mark Medina • February 9, 2016

CLEVELAND—The two stars laughed with each other as LeBron James bantered along with Kobe Bryant by the scorer's table. Bryant later teased James at center-court moments after he bricked an alley oop. Once the buzzer sounded, Bryant and James hugged each other and offered encouraging words.

The matchup Bryant and James shared last year at Staples Center conveyed the images of two close friends relishing both their tight bond and respect for each other's craft.

"They were smiling at each other," Cleveland guard Kyrie Irving recalled.

When the Lakers (11-43) visit the Cleveland Cavaliers (37-14) on Wednesday at Quicken Loans Arena, more nostalgia seems likely to emerge. After all, Bryant has savored seemingly every moment surrounding his 20th and final NBA season. James told reporters the game will become "very emotional just knowing it's his last hurrah."

"He's done so much, not only for the Lakers organization, but for me as a kid," James told reporters this week. "Growing up, I was watching Kobe and things

of that nature and also competing against him."

The Lakers technically list Bryant as questionable to play because of soreness in his right shoulder. But there is no question plenty expect him to play. Assuming that happens, Bryant and James appear likely to share moments that will include words, hugs and even matching up. But neither will be able to say with a straight face that they were always close.

James declined to tell reporters how his relationship with Bryant has evolved. But Bryant admitted last season he would not have shown such warmth toward James under different circumstances.

"If we were contending for a championship, I would be my same moody self," Bryant said. "But right now, I tend to have a little more perspective knowing I won't get a chance to play him on the court for much longer. You want to enjoy it."

Keeping a Distance

James gushed he sported an afro growing up because Bryant wore that look. James also had a poster of Bryant hanging in his room. Two days before playing in the NBA All-Star game in 2002, Bryant saw a 17-year-old

Kobe Bryant soars in for the dunk while LeBron James challenges him during the 2011 NBA All-Star Game. (AP Images)

James. The previous summer in New Jersey, Bryant spoke to James at ABCD Camp and gave him a pair of his signature shoes.

But once James followed Bryant's path in 2003 by jumping straight from high school to the NBA, any connection they had stopped there.

On the night James was drafted in 2003, Bryant upstaged his big night amid breaking news that he planned to opt out of his contract with the Lakers and seek free agency after the following season. In 2010, former Lakers coach Phil Jackson suspected Bryant did that to upstage James.

"He had to be the best every single night," said Cleveland coach Tyronn Lue, who played with Bryant from 1998-2001. "He's not going to open up to him and give him any leeway or give him any reason to try to come in and take his spot."

A relationship eventually developed on the 2008 U.S. Olympic team. Then, James got a first-hand look at Bryant's work ethic. Then, Bryant saw how James related to teammates to help elevate their play. In a joint interview on NBA Entertainment, Bryant praised James' athleticism while James complimented Bryant's fundamentals.

"There's a mutual respect that we have for one another," Bryant said. "It's that level of respect that enables us to perform at a high level when we compete against each other."

Yet, that respect mostly came from afar. So much that James admitted last year Bryant did not recruit him when the Lakers pursued him during the 2014 offseason.

Lost Opportunity

The matchup seemed inevitable. At least, that's what the Nike puppet commercials suggested.

Though most in the league anticipated James and Bryant meeting in the NBA Finals, something else happened. The Magic eliminated the Cavaliers in the 2009 Eastern Conference Finals. Cleveland's season ended early the following year with a loss to Boston in the Eastern semifinals. Meanwhile, Bryant's next two championships without Shaq happened against a forgettable team (Orlando) and an old rival (Boston).

"I know the world wanted to see it," James said earlier this season. "He held up his end and I didn't hold up my end, and I hate that."

Bryant did not hold up his end, either.

When James announced he would take his talents to South Beach for the 2010-11 season, Bryant recalled thinking, "I've got to get my knee healthy." But Bryant's knee stayed troublesome amid the Lakers' four-game loss to the Dallas Mavericks in the Western Conference semifinals. Dallas then humbled the Heat in the Finals.

While James won two NBA championships in four more NBA Finals appearances, the Lakers soon spiraled downward, partly amid endless injuries to Bryant.

"That makes me appreciate what I grew up watching with Magic (Johnson) and (Larry) Bird," said Bryant, referring to the Lakers and Celtics playing against each other in the NBA Finals three times in the 1980s. "You wanted to have that same kind of rivalry. But it never happened."

An Appreciation

The details stayed fresh in Lue's mind regarding a story that perfectly captures Bryant's competitiveness. During the 1999-2000 season, Lue blocked Bryant's layup attempt during a five-on-five scrimmage that left Bryant fuming.

"He went crazy. Kobe wanted to fight me at first.

Los Angeles Lakers' Kobe Bryant greets Cleveland Cavaliers' LeBron James before the start of their last match-up, on March 10, 2016, in Los Angeles. (AP Images)

Then he wanted to play one-on-one after practice," Lue said, smiling. "I said, 'No, I'm not playing you one-on-one.' He was so mad. After that, every day we stepped onto the court, he just went after me every single day."

Lue then described Bryant and Michael Jordan as a "spitting image of each other" after also playing with Jordan on the Washington Wizards (2001-2003). Does James have those same qualities?

"LeBron's the same way, it's just they're more vocal about it," Lue said. "They're more demonstrative about it. They'll get on guys. They'll cuss guys out. They'll even fight guys if they have to, so that's just the difference, but they still all have the same will to win."

Lue also argued they react the same way to other things, too. He reported that Bryant responded well to Jackson holding him and O'Neal "more accountable than anyone else on the team." Only two weeks into his head-coaching tenure, Lue said he critiqued James during film sessions and timeouts. As the 37-year-old Bryant has nursed season-long injuries the past three years, the 30-year-old James has changed his recovery and dietary habits.

Yet, Lue considers James' basketball IQ superior to anyone else, including Bryant and Jordan.

"With their will to win and the way they got on guys, they would fight a guy if they had to," Lue said. "But LeBron, his IQ (is better) because he can play 1, 2, 3, 4 and 5. And he knows every position on the floor."

Apparently, that would not have been possible without Bryant's influence from afar.

"I knew I had to be better because of Kobe Bryant," James said this season. "I knew he was in the gym and I knew he was working on his game. So every day that I didn't want to work out or every day I felt like I couldn't give more, I always thought of Kobe. Because I knew that he was getting better and I was like, 'Man, if you take a day off, he's going to take advantage of it.'"

All of which spurred a distant relationship into moments both Bryant and James will cherish on the court in Cleveland for one last time. ■

Kobe and LeBron stand side-by-side during LeBron's rookie year in 2004. They had many memorable battles throughout the years but never met in the NBA Finals. (L.A. Daily News: Hans Gutknecht)

Kobe Contemplates Passing the Torch

Lakers' Kobe Bryant Serves as Mentor for Several NBA's Young Stars, Role Players

By Mark Medina • December 14, 2014

His pre-draft workout just ended, leaving Nick Young with one responsibility that has become as natural as his infectious smile. He talked.

But reporters did not ask probing questions that often prompt Young to show off his goofy personality as a Lakers' reserve. Instead, Charlotte owner and NBA icon Michael Jordan peppered Young on various topics to evaluate how the former Cleveland High of Reseda and USC standout might fit on his roster.

Jordan eventually threw Young a curveball that both made him feel uncomfortable and compromise his allegiance to his childhood hero.

"He asked me where I learned my fadeaway from," Young recalled after working out for the former Charlotte Bobcats seven years ago. "Jordan was looking at me dead in my eyes. I was going to say Kobe Bryant, but I was forced to say Jordan at that moment because I wanted him to pick me."

When the Lakers (7-16) play the Minnesota Timberwolves (5-17) today at Target Center, Bryant will need to score only nine points to eclipse Jordan's 32,292 career points for third place on the NBA's all-time scoring list. Unsurprisingly, Bryant's upcoming milestone has fueled the never-ending comparisons to

Jordan, something that has followed Bryant throughout his 19-year career. But Young's uneasiness to Jordan's question provided a snapshot on how the current generation of NBA players idolize Bryant the same way the Lakers' 36-year-old star admires Jordan.

"It's so hard to compare anyone to Michael, but I think it's fair to say Kobe is the second coming of MJ," said Indiana Pacers forward Paul George, who grew up watching Bryant while playing for Knight High in Palmdale. "Kobe has transcended the league the same way I felt Michael did."

Idolizing Bryant

Bryant's presence struck a chord in different ways.

Cleveland forward LeBron James recently told reporters he had a Bryant poster on his bedroom wall growing up. The poster served as an inspiration for James as he followed Bryant's path in morphing from high school phenom to NBA star. Oklahoma City forward Kevin Durant told L.A. News Group last year he endlessly watched Bryant's scoring outbursts with hopes he could somehow replicate them.

George endlessly mimicked Bryant's mannerisms in pick-up games, ranging from his fadeaway jumpers to his jaw strutting. Golden State Warriors guard Klay

Kobe hugs Team USA teammate and fellow NBA superstar Chris Paul. They were nearly teammates on the Lakers in 2011 before the NBA rescinded the three-team trade with the Hornets and Rockets. (AP Images)

Thompson took similar notes, the former Santa Margarita standout often imitating Bryant's footwork and post-ups. Of course, plenty would love to reach Bryant's resume that entails five NBA championships, a career-high 81 points and the Lakers' all-time leading scorer.

"To get on his level is going to take a lot of work. It's basically impossible," Thompson said. "But he's never afraid to take the big shot, and that's what I've always tried to do."

Plenty of players have seen Bryant's offseason regimen that has helped maintain his prolific play and longevity.

NBA stars, such as James, Durant, Russell Westbrook, James Harden and Anthony Davis witnessed Bryant's routine during different stints with Team USA in the 2008 and 2012 Olympics. Both Thompson and Detroit Pistons guard Brandon Jennings attended Bryant's summer camps years before turning pro. Bryant's teammates, such as Young and Wesley Johnson, worked out privately with the Lakers' star this past summer.

All accounts tell the same story. Bryant's work day started at 5:00 a.m. He worked out without any interruptions. Bryant's approach involved repetitive drills on his footwork, shooting stroke and weight training.

"For a guy to be able to do that and still get ready for practice was pretty amazing," said Jennings, a Compton native. "That just made me want to work harder every day."

Memorable Interactions

Bryant proudly calls himself the "O.G. of the league," characterizing himself as the NBA's ambassador that imparts wisdom to any young star or role player willing to listen.

"I help them, mentor them and give them advice," Bryant said, "because I've pretty much seen it all."

Bryant has both exchanged text messages and talked extensively on the phone with Durant as late as 3 a.m, offering unspecified advice on how to improve his scoring and demand more out of his teammates. Bryant contacted George shortly after fracturing his right leg with USA Basketball this summer, offering sympathy and encouraging him to devote his on-court absence toward film study.

Washington Wizards guard John Wall, Thompson and Young report Bryant has provided positive reinforcement by praising their play and encouraging them to stay hungry.

"I always want to get better and I want to show my worth," Young said. "Playing on a team like Kobe and him taking me under his wing has been one of the best things for me."

Yet, Bryant still unleashes his on-court intensity on the same players he mentors.

In 2012, Bryant continuously jawed with Durant, Westbrook and Harden when they all played together in Oklahoma City during a regular-season game. Bryant did the same thing to Thompson during an exhibition game.

"I knocked into him in the lane and he told me if I did that again, he would knock my (butt) over," Thompson said. "I lit a fire under his belly. He has an edge at all times, even at the beginning of October. He wasn't messing around."

It appears Bryant welcomes the give-and-take.

Bryant and Young traded profanity-laced barbs during a recent practice. Young proclaimed, "Nobody in the world can guard me one-on-one." Bryant then

The 2015-2016 NBA season served as a farewell tour around the league for Kobe, but he also played the key role as mentor to young Lakers players, including franchise cornerstone D'Angelo Russell. (L.A. Daily News: Steve McCrank)

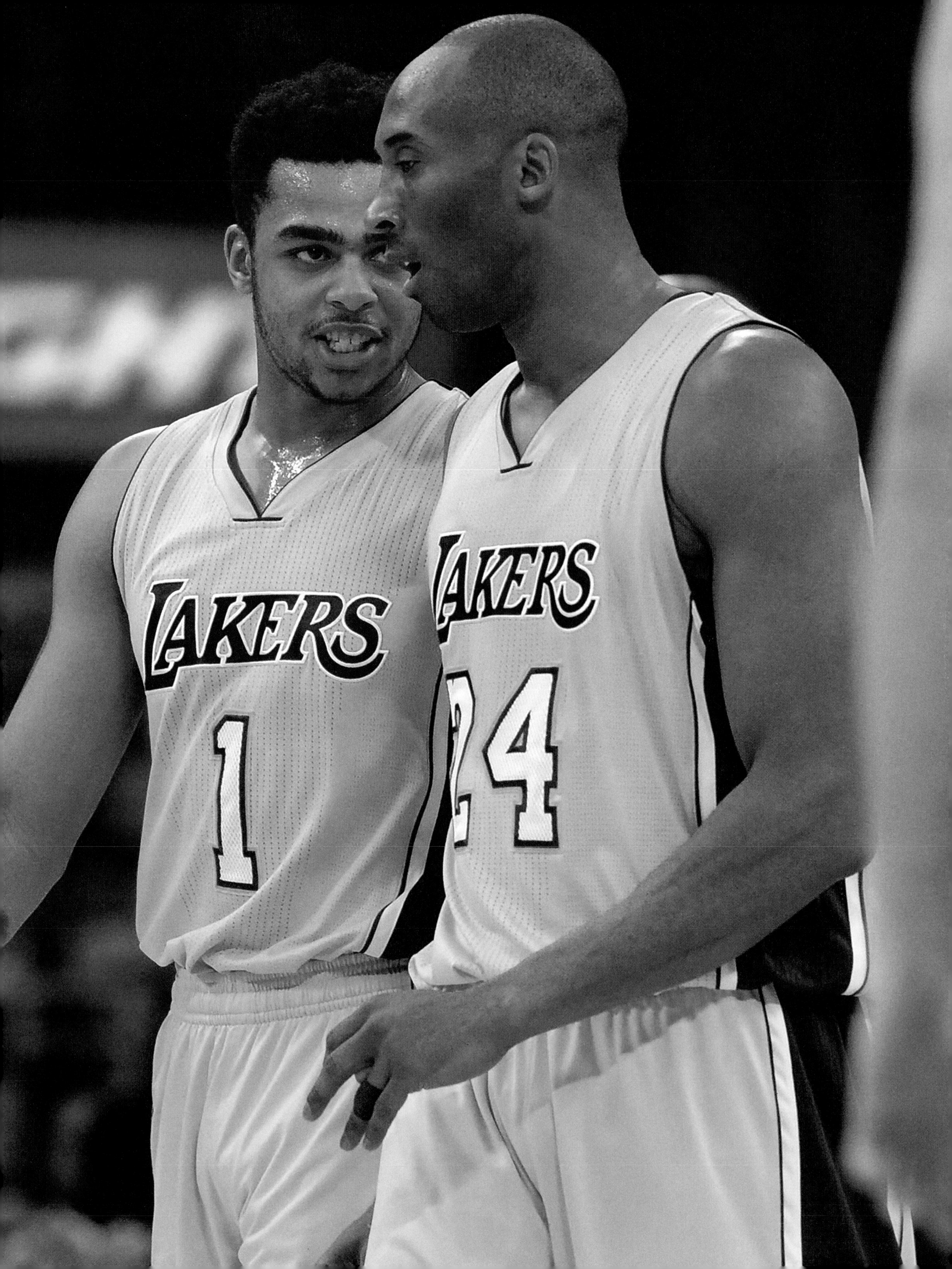
LAKERS
1
LAKERS
24

responded, "You're going exactly where I want you to go." Two years earlier at Team USA's pre-2012 Summer Olympic training camp in Las Vegas, Cleveland guard Kyrie Irving challenged Bryant to a game of one-on-one.

"I know your dad doesn't think you can beat me one-on-one," Bryant told Irving at the time. "Get your dad on the phone right now. Be like, 'Pops, I'm trying to bet Kobe 50 grand I can beat him one-on-one.' He'll be like, 'Son, are you crazy? Are you crazy?'"

Passing the Torch

Bryant may have embraced serving as the NBA's elderly statesman. But no rising star has become labeled as the next Bryant the same way the Lakers' star immediately sparked comparisons to Jordan.

"That door is closed. Good luck waiting on another Kobe Bryant," said ESPN analyst Jalen Rose. "The sport is his first, second and third priority."

Bryant expressed indifference on whether he will pass the torch to anyone. But he still believes he has served a purpose in instilling values that he believes has influenced the NBA's current generation that he described as "gym rats."

"The common denominator is always the competitive spirit, and how to get into that frame of mind night in and night out to go out and compete," Bryant said. "I grew up watching Michael. Michael grew up watching others play. So it's really just about watching, observing and learning from those that have come before you. You try to have that help you become a better basketball player." ■

Kobe and then Nuggets' forward Carmelo Anthony met in the 2009 Western Conference Finals, with the Lakers prevailing. The two are good friends, Olympic teammates and Melo has followed in Kobe's footsteps as one of the best scorers in the league. (L.A. Daily News: Hans Gutknecht)

A Very Kobe Christmas

Kobe Bryant's Top 5 Christmas Day Performances

By Brian Martin • December 23, 2015

Consider it the gift that keeps on giving. Kobe Bryant will be playing on Christmas Day for the 16th and final time when the Lakers host the Clippers in a 7:30 p.m. showdown.

While this is a game between local rivals, the competitiveness is up for debate. The Clippers have beaten the Lakers seven consecutive times and 11 of their past 12, with a margin of victory nearly 20 points.

Therefore, the best stare down Friday night might be between Father Time and the NBA's version of Father Christmas.

Despite Bryant missing the past two Christmas contests with injuries, no one has played more games that day. In fact, pick any day on the calendar, and none has featured Kobe Bryant in an NBA uniform more than Dec. 25.

On top of that, no one has scored more Christmas Day points than Bryant, who reached 383 in 2012 to surpass Oscar Robertson's record of 377.

In his 20th season, Bryant has had his struggles. But lately, it's as if the 38-year-old Lakers star has pulled a rabbit out of Santa's sack.

After dropping 31 points on Denver on Tuesday night, Bryant is averaging 20.6 points on 48.2 percent shooting in his past eight games going into Wednesday night's game against Oklahoma City.

So which Kobe Bryant is dropping down the Staples Center chimney Friday? That remains to be seen.

For now, fire up the chestnuts and pour yourself some egg nog.

Here are Bryant's five most memorable Christmas Day performances:

2008: Lakers 92, Boston 83

Just six months prior, the Lakers were reeling from their 39-point Game 6 thrashing at the hands of the NBA champion Celtics.

Here came Boston again, its Big Three of Paul Pierce, Kevin Garnett and Ray Allen boasting a 27-2 record and looking like shoo-ins for another title.

Bryant had other ideas. Playing a game-high 43 minutes, Bryant shot 13 of 23 for 27 points to go with nine rebounds and five assists.

And less than seven months later, it was Bryant & Co. calling themselves NBA champions.

2004: Miami 104, Lakers 102 (OT)

Dripping in drama, this marked the return of a vengeful Shaquille O'Neal and his first faceoff against the Lakers since he was traded to Miami.

Lakers fans got a load of a slimmed-down and bulked-up Shaq, who stuffed Bryant on his first drive to the rim. And after that, the heat was definitely on.

Kobe always brought something special for the big TV audience on Christmas Day games as the all-time leading scorer in those marquee match-ups. (L.A. Daily News: Hans Gutknecht)

Shaq finished with 24 points and 11 rebounds before fouling out. Dwyane Wade saved Miami's hide with a 29-point effort.

Yet it was Bryant who had a shot at the end clank off the rim, his 42 points and six assists all for naught.

Worth noting: Rounding out the Lakers starting five? Lamar Odom, Chris Mihm, Jumaine Jones and Chucky Atkins.

2007: Lakers 122, Phoenix 115

This one was fun.

Led by Steve Nash, Amare Stoudemire and Shawn Marion, Phoenix was loaded and could run.

As if further motivation was needed, the Suns ousted the Lakers from the first round of the playoffs the two previous seasons.

Bryant and the Lakers were up to the challenge. Buoyed by Andrew Bynum's career-high 28 points, the Lakers pulled away in the second half upon the shoulders of Bryant.

He scored 15 points in the third quarter, capped by a 3-pointer and reverse dunk in the final 33 seconds.

Bryant finished with a game-high 38 points to go with five rebounds and seven assists.

2009: Cleveland 102, Lakers 87

Yes, another loss and a blowout at that.

But if there's anything the NBA loves about its Christmas clashes, it's intrigue and star power.

This one had both. Kobe Bryant vs. LeBron James. And the Cavaliers had some center by the last name of O'Neal.

Bryant wound up with 35 points, nine rebounds and eight assists, shooting 11 of 33 from the field but 12 of 12 from the line.

Yet it was Bryant with the last laugh. He was hoisting the Larry O'Brien NBA Championship Trophy in June.

2012: Lakers 100, New York 94

This is the last time Bryant played Christmas Day.

East met West as the Lakers, stacked with Bryant, Pau Gasol, Dwight Howard and Steve Nash, came out on top after a rough start to the season.

Under new coach Mike D'Antoni, the Lakers defeated the Knicks for their fifth consecutive win to pull even at 14-14.

Bryant racked up 34 points to match New York's Carmelo Anthony. It was the ninth game in a row in which Bryant, who shot 14 of 24 (58.3 percent), scored at least 30. ■

Showman that he was, Lakers fans could always count on a great performance from Kobe on Christmas Day. (L.A. Daily News: David Crane)

Dunking with the Stars

Kobe Bryant Opens up about Storied NBA All-Star History

By Mark Medina • February 14, 2016

TORONTO—Practice stopped abruptly. Then, players, coaches and fans watched something on the Ricoh Coliseum scoreboard that has caught everybody's attention for almost two decades.

Highlights of Kobe Bryant's All-Star performances played on a loop. They showed how Bryant collected four All-Star MVPs to tie Bob Pettit for a league record. They showed how Bryant set an NBA All-Star-record 280 points.

When Bryant plays his final All-Star game on Sunday at Air Canada Centre, will the Lakers' 37-year-old star provide another highlight?

"My storybook ending would be to enjoy this experience and help these young guys," said Bryant, who wants to play around 10 minutes. "It's important for them to take advantage of the moment."

Hence, Bryant did not sound thrilled when Golden State Warriors guardStephen Curry told him, "I have a lot of assists for you."

"I said, 'No. What are you doing? You're a shooter,'" Bryant said. "You grew up watching me. What the hell are you talking about that you want to pass me the ball at an All-Star game? Are you crazy?"

It also remains crazy to fathom how Bryant's NBA All-Star history marked defining moments of his 20-year NBA career.

"He has so many great memories and there's so much great footage," Cleveland forward LeBron James said. "I don't know how you guys will able to mix, match and put together his legacy."

The Beginning

Bryant's favorite All-Star memory starts with his rookie season. In 1997, Bryant gushed about talking with Michael Jordan, Clyde Drexler, Charles Barkley and John Stockton.

"They were probably like, 'Who is this kid? It's just extremely annoying, because he just keeps asking all these questions,'" Bryant said. "But the guys that came before me shared so much insight."

That could have helped Bryant with his first All-Star accomplishment. Bryant won the 1997 NBA Slam Dunk Contest by performing an in-between-the-legs dunk.

"I didn't want to do it. I was too nervous," Bryant said, laughing. "But I wound up having fun and winning the thing."

The Start

Bryant was not considered good enough to start for the Lakers in 1998. But the 19-year-old Bryant was considered good and popular enough to become the youngest player to start in an All-Star game.

That pitted Bryant against Jordan, and the Lakers'

Kobe dunks during the second quarter of the 2005 NBA All-Star game in Denver, one of 18 All-Star Games that he was chosen for. (AP Images)

young star appeared eager to accomplish one thing.

"Going up against him and defending the turnaround shot," Bryant said. "During the regular season, I didn't get a chance to match up with him too much in that regard. In the All-Star game, I had a chance to measure it, see the tempo of it, the footwork of it and physicality of it. It was fun."

It was also fun for Jordan and Bryant to trade baskets. Jordan won his third All-Star MVP after posting 23 points on 10-of-18 shooting. Bryant had 18 points on 7-of-16 shooting, six rebounds and two steals despite sitting in the fourth quarter.

"I got blamed for Kobe not getting the MVP because I took him out," said Sacramento coach George Karl, who coached the Western Conference All-Stars that year. "I couldn't believe that."

But Karl confirmed Karl Malone asked to sit amid frustration with Bryant.

"Karl said to take him out because Kobe told him to get off the block," Karl said. "He said, 'Get out of my way.'"

The Boos

The moment in 2002 seemed too perfect for Bryant to receive a standing ovation. He collected his first All-Star MVP. He posted 31 points in his Philadelphia hometown.

But instead of showering Bryant with brotherly love, Philadelphia fans booed him both throughout the game and during the MVP ceremony. After all, Bryant helped the Lakers beat the Sixers in the 2001 NBA Finals.

"It gave me a stronger will and more motivation to be a great player," Bryant said. "It gave me a stronger sense of a killer instinct."

Be Like Mike

Bryant already had a killer instinct partly because of studying Jordan. So when Bryant guarded in Jordan's final All-Star game in 2003, it seemed inevitable they would chirp.

"That was a foul all day long," Jordan said.

"I know you ain't talking," Bryant replied.

"You only got three [rings]. I got six," Jordan responded. "That's why I should get that foul."

Nearly 13 years later, Bryant had no comeback.

"The ring count is one I can't catch," Bryant conceded after winning five NBA titles.

But after Jordan made a potential game-winning fade-away jumper in the 2003 All-Star game with 4.8 seconds left in overtime, Bryant drew a foul on the next possession and forced double overtime. Bryant then scored 55 points on Jordan that season, a feat Bryant once reminded Jordan about years later during All-Star weekend.

"That's how I showed respect to MJ," Bryant said. "I take the things I learn from them and the competitive spirit from them, and give it back."

The Feud

After fighting over roles and personality differences, the feud between Bryant and Shaquille O'Neal became an inevitable storyline during All-Star weekend.

In 2004 at Staples Center, O'Neal won the All-Star MVP award over Bryant. After the Lakers traded O'Neal the following summer to Miami, Bryant and O'Neal ignored each other in the 2005 All-Star game during pre-game handshakes. In 2007, Bryant stole the spotlight from O'Neal by winning his second All-Star MVP award.

Yet, Bryant said he and O'Neal "were always civil." O'Neal insisted their lack of interactions as opposing All-Stars "was never anything personal." The two proved that publicly when Bryant and O'Neal (then with the Phoenix Suns) shared the All-Star MVP award in 2009.

"That moment really broke the ice," said O'Neal, who relished Bryant giving the trophy to his son, Shareef. "After that, I knew all the stuff we went through was silly."

Bryant viewed that episode differently, saying they

Kobe goes up for the reverse layup during the 2004 NBA All-Star Game in Los Angeles, at his home court of Staples Center. (AP Images)

had already become "extremely friendly."

"When you put two guys in a locker room every single day and have complete differences on how you should get somewhere, you're going to have confrontation," Bryant said. "Now that we go our separate ways and see each other only once every whenever, that's great."

Capturing Los Angeles

The Lakers unveiled Jerry West's statue outside Staples Center. Clippers forward Blake Griffin won the Slam Dunk Contest by jumping over a car. But Bryant still owned All-Star weekend in Los Angeles in 2011.

Bryant had his hand and feet immersed at the Grauman's Chinese Theater. He then left another imprint by collecting his fourth All-Star MVP with 37 points on 14 of 26 shooting and 14 rebounds.

"He told me early in the game, he'll try to get a feel if he can go for the MVP by how his shots were falling," said Chicago Bulls forward and former Lakers teammate Pau Gasol. "He does that because he's so ambitious and wants to be the best."

So much that Griffin and Kevin Love teased Bryant for stealing their rebounds. Bryant responded, "I'm the double-double king."

"Being around so many young players," Bryant said, "gave me so much energy by seeing them bounce around."

Taking The Pain

The replay shows Miami Heat guard Dwyane Wade accidentally broke Bryant's nose in the 2012 All-Star game. The medical tests show Bryant suffered a mild concussion.

Bryant stayed in the game and scored 27 points to surpass Jordan's previous All-Star record in points scored (271). On the final play, Bryant also defended James and forced him to pass. In the 2013 NBA All-Star game, Bryant also blocked James twice. James joked, "I was injured."

But it was Bryant who was injured in 2012, though he did not play like it.

"You get a shot from somebody, the last thing you want them to know is they took you out," Bryant said. "You have to hit me harder than that."

Wade hit Bryant hard enough that Bryant needed to wear a plastic mask. A week later, Bryant scored 33 points against the Heat.

"There were no hard feelings," said Wade, who apologized privately to Bryant. "But I expected him to come out and give me what he did."

The Injuries

Bryant could not overcome all injuries during All-Star weekend. He stayed sidelined in 2010 (left ankle), 2014 (left knee) and 2015 (right shoulder). Bryant also only played three minutes in 2008. Bryant called those moments "extremely frustrating."

"You can sit there, whine, complain and feel sorry for yourself," Bryant said. "But that's not going to do anything about it. You have to move quickly to a place of acceptance and figure out what you can do."

The Last Chapter

Bryant has figured out enough to stay healthy to play in his 15th All-Star game and making his 18th All-Star appearance. That already has created more memories.

Jordan presented Bryant with his entire Nike catalog, which includes 30 of Jordan's various shoes in brilliant white.

"I told him, 'You have no idea how much I worked to try to find a pair of shoes when I was in high school," Bryant said. "Now I have the whole collection. It's pretty sweet."

So is the possibility that Bryant could make more All-Star memories once he steps on the court. ∎

Bryant poses with the MVP trophy for the 2011 NBA All-Star Game in Los Angeles, one of four All-Star MVP wins for Kobe. He had 37 points and 14 rebounds, both game highs. (L.A. Daily News: David Crane)

Kobe's All-Star Farewell

Bryant Just Wants to Relish Final All-Star Game Moment

By Mark Medina • February 12, 2016

TORONTO—The noise became louder with every move Kobe Bryant made.

He stood up from a press table and groaned. Bryant moved his feet and winced. Bryant then uttered "Oh God," before stepping from the platform to the ground. He then walked gingerly after sitting for almost 12 minutes.

Moments earlier, the Lakers' 37-year-old star provided a sober analysis on the state of his body.

"I feel horrible," Bryant said following the Lakers' loss to Cleveland on Wednesday at Quicken Loans Arena. "Seriously. My ankles, knees, everything. This stretch couldn't come at a better time."

It could be better, though.

The Lakers (11-43) will rest during the nearly week-long NBA All-Star break that started Thursday and concludes on Wednesday. Coach Byron Scott will vacation in Mexico. Forward Julius Randle will relax in the Bahamas. And other players will stay in Los Angeles.

But Bryant will spend the first part of the break participating here in NBA All-Star weekend. He will start for the Western Conference on Sunday at Air Canada Centre in what marks his 18th selection to the All-Star game. That marks the second-most selections behind the 19 All-Star games former Lakers center Kareem Abdul-Jabbar played.

As another reminder of his aging body, Bryant will appear in his first All-Star game after missing the previous two because of season-ending injuries to his left knee and right shoulder, respectively.

Bryant's itinerary will also remain endless, with countless media and endorsement obligations today and Saturday.

"It is busy, but it's also very selective," Bryant said. "So there's certain things that we'll do that's short bursts of appearances. But nothing too long. Nothing where I'm on my feet for long periods of time."

In between, Bryant plans to receive endless treatment that will include ice baths, massages and rest. He will also stay with his family at a hotel different than the one accommodating other NBA All-Stars, both to maximize recovery time and to maximize privacy. Bryant then pointed out he will have days off on Monday and Tuesday, during which he will "do nothing."

Scott joked he will watch Sunday's game only if "they got the game on the golf course on the 15th hole." Scott also joked that he will text San Antonio coach Gregg Popovich not to play Bryant 37 minutes, considering the Lakers will then play next Friday against the Spurs at Staples Center.

Kobe addresses the crowd while fellow Lakers legend Magic Johnson and his All-Star contemporaries look on. The 2015 All-Star Game in Toronto was the last of his storied career. (AP Images)

"Pop is great," Scott said. "I don't worry about that."

But Scott did worry enough about Bryant to voice concerns to him before parting ways during the break.

"'I know you're not going to get a bit of sleep,'" Scott recalled saying. "'I know it's going to be very taxing on you. Everybody wants to pay a tribute to you in some form or fashion.'"

And then there's the game itself.

Bryant has accomplished plenty, with four All-Star MVPs (2002, 2007, 2009 and 2011). He has set All-Star game records for points scored (280), most field goals made (115) and most steals (37, tied with Michael Jordan). But amid Bryant's last season, TNT analyst and former Lakers teammate Shaquille O'Neal suspected Bryant will try to collect an All-Star record fifth MVP award to surpass Bob Pettit.

"If he can find his stroke and get it going a little bit, I can guarantee you he's going to go for the MVP," O'Neal said in a conference call this week. "It's his last one. Why not go out with a bang?"

Bryant reacted to O'Neal's argument with the same dismissiveness as when they butted heads over their respective roles in their eight years together on the Lakers (1996-2004).

"Why? I'm good. I'm good. I'm good," Bryant said. "I'll make a couple jump shots and try to play the best I can. But I'm OK."

Bryant's eyes then lit up and his tone softened when he spoke giddily about what he wants to experience in his last All-Star game.

"Enjoy being around the guys," Bryant said. "Seriously, this is crazy. This is 20 years for me, that's more than half my life playing in the NBA and being in the locker room."

Bryant then noted he could have "babysat" Golden State guard Stephen Curry when Bryant first entered the NBA. Bryant remarked he knew Warriors guard Klay Thompson "when he was a young kid." Bryant expressed giddiness on appearing in his eighth All-Star game with Cleveland forward LeBron James and his fourth All-Star appearance with Oklahoma City forward Kevin Durant.

"I can't wait to be around them and just talk to them and see how far the game has progressed and seeing all this young talent and the different generations of players," Bryant said. "I'll be able to sit in the locker room and seriously just look at it all and just smile and just take it all in."

By that point, Bryant's nostalgia amid the adulation from peers and fans may overwhelm him enough that he will not think about the pain he currently nurses. ■

Kobe Bryant reacts to the crowd as he leaves the game during second half of NBA All-Star action in Toronto. Teammate and Golden State Warriors superstar Stephen Curry looks on and claps. (AP Images)

Philadelphia Roots

Kobe Bryant's Storied Legacy, Both Good and Bad

By Mark Medina • February 6, 2014

PHILADELPHIA—This should've marked the time when Kobe Bryant would stroll into his hometown and revisit the foundation that spurred his greatness.

He would've spent the Lakers' day off Thursday stopping at Lower Merion, a suburban high school just outside Philadelphia which he led to a state championship title in 1996 (its first in 53 years) and broke Wilt Chamberlain's Southeastern Pennsylvania high school scoring record (2,883 to 2,252). Bryant would've given the current Aces a pep talk. Or perhaps Bryant would've stayed silent, as observers noticed last year, because of his want not to disrupt practice.

Bryant would've worked out at the school's old practice gym before grabbing a cheesesteak at Larry's (with ketchup, no onions or cheese) or a pepperoni pizza at Bella Italia Pizza (which showcases an autographed Bryant picture frame among various Italian soccer memorabilia), two food joints that reside only a few minutes away from Lower Merion and Bryant's old neighborhood in Wynnewood, Pa. Or perhaps he would've stayed strict to his recently revamped diet to maintain longevity.

Bryant then would've taken court when the Lakers (17-32) visit the Philadelphia 76ers (15-35) Friday night at Wells Fargo Center, where the Sixers fans would boo him. Memories remain fresh here of Bryant joining the Lakers shortly after graduating from high school and his subsequent clashes with the Sixers, most notably in the 2001 NBA Finals.

Instead, a fractured left knee has kept him sidelined on the court and away from the Lakers on their three-game trip, leaving Lower Merion without its most famous alum greeting them in the hallway and on the hardwood.

"It's disappointing. We always look forward toward seeing Kobe when he comes back into town," Lower Merion coach Gregg Downer said. "It has to be really hard on him to be on the sidelines having all of these injury issues. He's such a competitor that sitting on the bench is not in his DNA."

A recent trip to Philadelphia revealed Bryant's legacy here goes beyond his physical presence. Or the myriad of Bryant's accomplishments that includes five NBA championships, a fourth-place ranking on the NBA's all-time scoring list and countless game-winning baskets. Or Sonny Hill, an historian of Philadelphia basketball in part because of his 46-year-old Sonny Hill Community Involvement League that has boasted several NBA stars, ranking Bryant as Philadelphia's second best basketball player only behind Chamberlain because he broke numerous scoring records and prompted various rule changes.

Lower Merion and Bryant shaped each other toward unyielding excellence. Meanwhile, the city

Kobe guards Allen Iverson during Game 1 of the 2001 NBA Finals. Kobe's Lakers vanquishing the 76ers added to the complex feelings about Kobe in Philadelphia. (L.A. Daily News: Michael Owen Baker)

shares a nuanced view on Bryant's legacy.

"Kobe's regarded, justifiably so, as one of the greatest players out of Philadelphia. That in itself is greatness considering Philadelphia's basketball history," said Hill, who's also an executive advisor for the 76ers. "People in Philadelphia will always recognize his greatness. But they will identify the fact he's not playing for Philadelphia and will see it from that point of view."

Tales of the Hardwood

A drive through Bryant's neighborhood entails some landmarks that explain his ascension.

Turn onto Remington road and you will find Wynnewood Valley Park, where Bryant practiced day and night by himself on an unassuming basketball court. Drive a few minutes later toward Haverford road, and you will see the Kaiserman Jewish Community Center, where Bryant frequented for pickup games. Lower Merion High School features a refurbished gym Bryant donated in 2010 worth $500,000 that showcases his retired No. 33 jersey and the Aces' 1996 state championship trophy behind a glass case.

But what makes Bryant's name still resonate in these hallways involves stories that reveal his unmatched competitiveness, such as arriving to school to practice at 6 a.m., taking at least 1,000 shots per day and ensuring he wins every drill.

Shortly after living the past seven years in Italy, Bryant spent the summer of 1991 as a sixth grader in his first season at the Sonny Hill Community Involvement League. Hill doesn't recall Bryant's recent contention to Sports Illustrated that he didn't score a single basket that summer. But Hill noticed a young and scrawny Bryant appearing overwhelmed with the physical demands of the game. In subsequent years, Hill remembers stopping games to point out Bryant's superior fundamentals with his footwork and pull-up jumpers.

Once he reached eighth grade at nearby Bala Cynwd Middle School, Bryant worked out with the Lower Merion varsity team. It took Downer only five

minutes before he turned to an assistant and remarked Bryant would play in the NBA someday, a path his father (Joe "Jelly Bean Bryant") and uncle (Chubby Cox) once reached albeit without the same success. Teammates also recall Bryant making passing references into wanting to become the NBA's best player.

"I had this gauge for him where I'd say, 'Your pool right now is being among the top 100 high school kids in the country," Downer said. "Now your pool is 50 kids and then 25 kids. He kept meeting those checkpoints. I told him heading into his senior year, 'I want you to become a McDonald's All-American.' We talked about that when he was in ninth grade."

Bryant reached that plateau, providing endless moments teammates still remember vividly.

By his junior year during the 1994-95 season, Bryant had stomach flu in a regular-season game against Haverford, well before a certain idol named Michael Jordan famously played through one and scored 38 points in Game 5 of the 1997 NBA Finals against Utah .

"Kobe was throwing up before the game and he didn't come out with us for warmups," recalled Guy Stewart, one of Bryant's former teammates and a current assistant at Lower Merion. "During the game, he wasn't showing many symptoms. But I knew he felt weak. You could tell he wasn't himself. But he got himself together and still ended up with 45 points."

During his senior season, Bryant broke his nose after diving for a loose ball and colliding with a teammate named Leo Stacy. Leading up to the Aces' state semifinal game against rival Chester, Bryant tried on various masks to protect his tender nose. Bryant also donned a plastic mask after suffering a concussion during the 2011-12 season with the Lakers.

Moments before tipoff, accounts from Downer and Bryant's teammates describe him delivering a profanity-laced speech before throwing the mask against the wall. Bryant then led his team with 39 points in an overtime win that took the Aces to the state championship game.

"He was determined if he wore the mask, he

Bryant goes up for the shot against 76ers big man Dikembe Mutombo in Game 2 of the 2001 NBA Finals. (L.A. Daily News: John Lazar)

wouldn't be able to see and breathe the same," said Jermaine Griffin, a former Bryant teammate at Lower Merion. "Anytime you got your best player showing no fear and not letting anything hold him back, that fuels the fire for everybody."

Bryant unleashed his intensity out on high school teammates long before he did so with his current ones. He chewed out a benchwarmer in practice for taking a last-second shot in a three-on-three drill instead of passing Bryant the ball, a sequence that cost his team the game.

"I could feel him glaring at me from behind. I'm trying not to look at him, but he kept saying something and sounded legitimately angry," said Rob Schwartz, then a 5-foot-7 junior. "He kept charging me. I ran as fast as I could out of the gym and out into the hallway until I realized he wasn't chasing me anymore."

But the Aces attribute Bryant's intensity as crucial in the Aces' rise from his freshman year (4-20), sophomore season (20-6), junior season (26-5, state quarterfinals) and senior season (31-3, state championship). A short time later Bryant announced, "I have decided to skip college and take my talents to the NBA."

A Lasting Impact

More than 18 years later, Bryant casts a looming shadow on the program.

Two mosaic portraits of Bryant and the 1996 state title team permeate the Lower Merion High School hallway. A billboard-sized banner in the school's refurbished gym titled "Bryant Gymnasium" features Bryant and his teammates hoisting the 1996 championship trophy. Lower Merion High school spokesman Doug Young, who was a senior on Bryant's team his sophomore season, estimated he grants 10-15 informal tours to out-of-town guests eager to learn more about their favorite NBA star. That included 24-year-old Matt Starcevich, of Northwest Indiana, who coincidentally was in town to see a recent Jay-Z concert.

"I was asking my friend what is there to do in Philadelphia," Starcevich said. "He was telling me about

the Rocky steps, the Phillies' ballpark and all the stuff about American history. I was like, 'I really don't give a hoot about those things.'"

Instead, he wanted to learn about Bryant. Consider the feeling mutual around here.

Downer occasionally puts Bryant on speaker phone to talk to his players before a big game. Bryant has invited the team to watch his private workouts. The Aces' coaching staff and players help out Bryant at his annual summer camp in Santa Barbara. Bryant also donates Nike uniforms and shoes to the Aces' boys and girls basketball teams. Lower Merion fans occasionally taunt struggling Aces players with "You aren't Kobe" chants. In the Aces' recent win over rival Consetoga, Lower Merion boasted a fast-paced system that thrives on fast-breaks layups, swift ball movement and disciplined man-to-man defense, the same tenets the Aces adopted when Bryant played for them.

"Kobe inspires us and talks to us about the culture of Lower Merion basketball," said Aces senior Justin McFadden, who's committed next year to Binghamton. "He always talks about how you have to play hard every minute and you have to work for your brothers. It makes you want to keep the legacy going."

Bryant's coaches and teachers show equal passion.

Downer staunchly disputed rumors former Lakers coach Phil Jackson floated a decade ago that Bryant intentionally sabotaged games at Lower Merion so he could close the game with a memorable finish.

"I was upset by that. I never had the opportunity to meet Phil, and I would've liked to. But It was such an uneducated comment and they weren't even true," Downer said. "Kobe knows I have his back and vice versa."

With the Lakers trailing the Boston Celtics, 3-2, in the 2010 NBA Finals, Bryant's English teacher, Jeanne Mastriano, left an emotional voice mail that lasted three minutes and praised his skill and resilience. The Lakers won that series in seven games, with Mastriano's message inspiring Bryant.

"I saved that message," Mastriano recalls Bryant

Kobe's Bryant looks to Jermaine Griffin, right, the co-captain from his senior year of basketball at Lower Merion High School, as Bryant's high school jersey number, 33, is hoisted up to the top of the Lower Merion High School gym and retired in January, 2002, in Ardmore, Pa. (AP Images)

telling her. "I played it over and over and over again when I was getting ready for the next game."

Despite Downer saying in jest the Aces "were a Kobe Bryant ankle sprain from being an average team," he and his players point to the team's success following his departure as evidence the program doesn't solely rely on Bryant's legacy. Likewise, Young said Lower Merion followed Bryant's instructions not to make its refurbished gym into what he called "a shrine." The rest of the gym showcases billboard-sized photographs depicting the rest of Lower Merion's athletic teams.

Lower Merion won three consecutive Central League titles after Bryant graduated. The Aces appeared in four state championship games (2005, 2006, 2012, 2013) and won two of them (2006, 2013). Downer characterizes himself as taking a balanced approach in telling stories about Bryant's heroics. He touts his accomplishments as teachable moments, yet tries to scale back in hopes his players feel more empowered to carve their own path.

"He created a culture of winning and a culture of hard work that I saw first-hand," Downer said. "He raised the bar with how hard you have to work. In our own, way we've been able to sustain that. It's like a snowball rolling down low. You want to keep it going. When Kobe leaves, you don't want to become tiny."

A Different View

Philadelphia hardly has shown Bryant much brotherly love, however.

An informal sampling among those in and outside Lower Merion provide plenty of reasons.

Lower Merion is considered a plush suburban school about 20 minutes west of Philadelphia. Bryant jumped to the NBA instead of attending a local school, such as Villanova or LaSalle. The Sixers used their No. 1 draft pick in 1996 to select Allen Iverson while the Lakers traded Vlade Divac to Charlotte to secure the rights to its 13th pick that went for Bryant. He routinely dons Yankees or Dodgers caps instead of the Phillies.

When the Lakers' played the Sixers in the 2001 NBA Finals, Bryant said he wanted "to cut their hearts out."

That prompted Sixers fans to boo him loudly when Bryant hoisted the 2002 All-Star MVP trophy in Philadelphia. He's routinely booed in regular-season games, too.

"If one of our players said, 'I'm going to cut their hearts out,' we'd be running up and throwing a parade for him," said Jim Fenerty, the director of athletics for Germantown Academy, a private suburban school outside of Philadelphia. "But this is him playing for the Lakers and he's saying this about his hometown."

Plenty of Bryant's supporters remain frustrated with the apparent hypocrisy.

"Kobe embodies everything that Philadelphia ball players want to have in their stars," said Evan Monsky, a former Bryant teammate at Lower Merion. "He plays hurt. He's gritty as hell. He's not scared. He goes to the rack. He's a winner."

That's why there's some sentiment inside and outside the Aces' program that the city's attitude relatively softened toward Bryant.

He still fields boos when he plays the Sixers, but Bryant also has sparked cheers. That happened when Bryant eclipsed former teammate and adversary Shaquille O'Neal two years ago on the NBA's all-time scoring list. Bryant received some "M-V-P" chants toward the end of the Lakers' win last year in Philadelphia after scoring 34 points.

But without Bryant's presence with the Lakers on the latest trip, it remains to be seen how vocal the local displeasure would've been this time around. But as Bryant nears the tail end of his career, it's possible the final chapters on his legacy here remains unwritten.

"When you speak to him about Philadelphia you will find that he will say if not for Philadelphia, he wouldn't be the player he is today," Hill said. "The only way you can change more of his perception is if he becomes more involved in Philadelphia away from basketball after his career. That's his call." ∎

Philadelphia 76ers Hall of Famer Julius "Dr. J" Erving, left, presents Kobe Bryant with his Lower Merion high school uniform prior to the game in December, 2015, at Wells Fargo Center in Philadelphia. (USA TODAY Sports)

Beef Squashed

Kobe & Shaq Bury Hatchet During Podcast

By Mark Medina • August 31, 2015

The detente started when Shaquille O'Neal introduced his long-time adversary with words of affection.

"The greatest Laker ever," O'Neal said, "Mr. Kobe Bryant."

The detente ended when O'Neal said goodbye to Bryant with a message that equally waxed nostalgia, gratitude and remorse amid three NBA championship runs, endless bickering and a messy divorce.

"Kobe, I just wanted to say I love you brother," O'Neal said. "I miss you. I enjoyed the times we played together. I wish we could have gotten to seven championships. But it is what it is. We're still the most respected and most dominant one-two punch in Lakers history."

It also appears that Bryant and O'Neal are still one of the most talked about duos in Lakers history.

Bryant and O'Neal have not played together since the Lakers traded O'Neal in 2004 after the team's NBA Finals loss to Detroit. Yet, plenty of intrigue remains surrounding O'Neal's relationship with Bryant. So much that the two appeared on "The Big Podcast with Shaq" for an episode released on Monday. For nearly 30 minutes, both O'Neal and Bryant spoke with equal candor about their respect for their game and the never-ending personality tensions.

"It's time to clear the air. We were the most enigmatic, controversial and most talked about dominant one-two punch," O'Neal said. "I want people to know I don't hate you. I know you don't hate me. I called it a work beef. I was young. You were young. But as I look at it, we won three out of four [championships]. So I don't really think a lot was done wrong. So I just wanted to clear the air and let everyone know, 'No, I don't hate you.' We had a lot of disagreements. We had a lot of arguments. But I think it both fueled us."

The arguments seemed plenty.

O'Neal griped about Bryant's high-volume shooting. Bryant complained about O'Neal's work ethic and conditioning. The "two alpha males," as O'Neal put it, both seemed intent on fighting for the team's dominant role.

O'Neal expressed regret for publicly demanding a trade, though former Lakers owner Jerry Buss proved the driving force in his departure. Bryant wished the two had not become so open about their differences to the media. Yet, neither sounded remorseful about their once contentious relationship.

"I'm not really a nostalgic person either to be honest with you. Shaq and I are much the same in the sense that we look at the jewelry that we won. You can't argue that," Bryant said. "What made [the arguments] special is we said them to each other's face. We didn't go behind each other's back and whisper to our teammates about this, that and the other. That can create friction

Shaq and Kobe are all smiles during the 2001 NBA Finals. (L.A. Daily News: John Lazar)

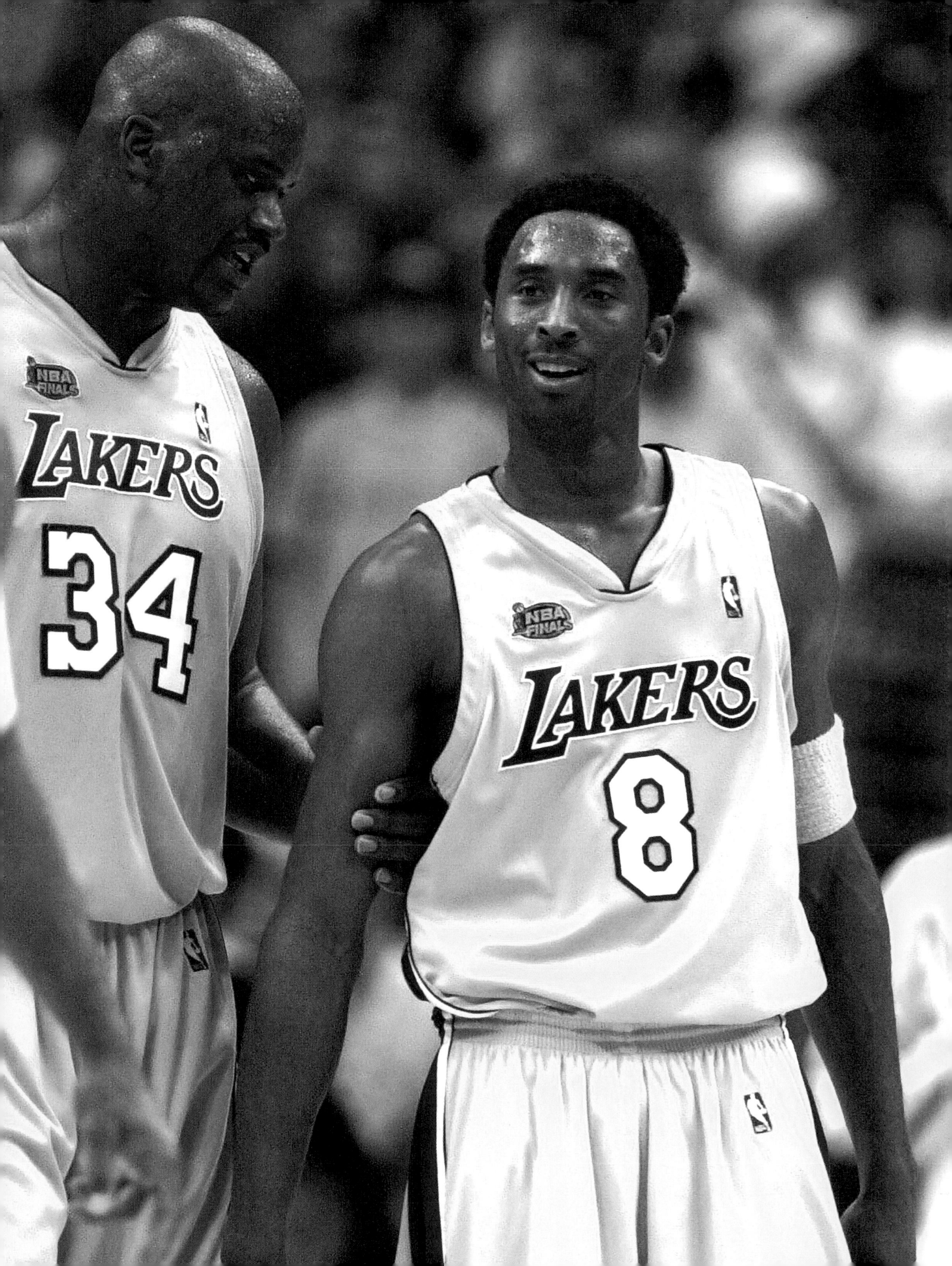
NBA FINALS
LAKERS
34
NBA FINALS
LAKERS
8

and become cancerous to the team. When you get things out in front of each other and you say what you're thinking and you have those disagreements, you agree to disagree and you move on. The integrity of the team is preserved. Then when we come out of it agreeing or whatever the case may be, then the team is all the more better for it. Now you have more momentum. That's what really catapulted us."

Bryant and O'Neal did not address certain events that contributed to their feud.

When Bryant was charged with an eventually dropped sexual assault in Eagle, Colo. in 2003, the police report quoted him as telling authorities that O'Neal had paid off unnamed mistresses with hush money. During that year's training camp, O'Neal downplayed his absence because of injuries and his impending trial, saying, "The full team is here. I want to be right for Derek [Fisher], Karl [Malone] and Gary [Payton]."

During that same season, O'Neal challenged Bryant to opt out of his contract if he did not like playing second fiddle to him. Bryant then had an interview with former ESPN reporter Jim Gray, criticizing O'Neal's leadership, work ethic and conditioning.

Yet, Bryant suggested the problems he had with O'Neal became inevitable amid the similar personality and mindset they had to score.

"How many years would Michael Jordan and Wilt Chamberlain be playing together with Wilt in his prime and Michael wanting to come up and grow?" Bryant asked. "How long is that going to last before Michael says, 'You know what? It's time for me to show what I can do.' It is what it is. That's why he and I are one of a kind when it comes to tandem because you literally have two alpha males playing together on one team and that normally does not happen."

O'Neal also did not mention how he alienated the late Jerry Buss. After making a basket a preseason game in Honolulu in 2003, O'Neal shouted to Buss, "Now you gonna pay me?" referring to a contract extension.

Buss did not provide that extension. Buss traded O'Neal to Miami on July 14, 2004 and re-signed Bryant the next day to a seven-year, $136 million deal. Buss has said he preferred a younger Bryant over an aging O'Neal, sensing that Bryant's play was just peaking while O'Neal would later become saddled with injuries.

"Dr. Buss called me and said, 'This is what we want to do and now this is what we're going to do. We have to trade you,'" O'Neal said. "I always have respected Dr. Buss for that. I have no problems or quarrels with his family. That's how you do business."

Bryant has also said in recent years that Jackson sided with O'Neal both to appease him and motivate Bryant. O'Neal once suggested Jackson partly instigated the tension with Bryant. Jackson also wrote a book titled "The Last Season," that had described Bryant as "uncoachable." Yet, both sides downplayed Jackson's role, so much that O'Neal said that Jackson had used Robert Horry as team's "whipping boy."

Said O'Neal: "He was really fair. He only got fed up one time where he came in and said, 'Both of you need to cut it out.' That's the only thing he said. It wasn't a catering situation."

Said Bryant: "Phil Jackson was even with how he handled it. He managed the team like a see saw."

But O'Neal and Bryant revealed two episodes that contributed to the animosity.

In 1999, O'Neal and Bryant fought each other in practice.

"He would either beat the [crap] out of me, or I would get a couple good ones in. I was comfortable with either one," Bryant said. "I probably had a couple of screws loose because I nearly got into a fistfight and

Kobe and Shaq clashed often during the time as Lakers teammates but their chemistry and success on the court was undeniable. (L.A. Daily News: Will Lester)

I actually was willing to get into a fight with this man. I went home and thought I'm either the dumbest or most courageous kid on the face of the Earth."

Reports suggested O'Neal took offense at the time that Bryant challenged his authority. But O'Neal looks at the situation the same way Bryant does.

"That showed me this kid was not going to back down," O'Neal said. "Kobe's seen me punk every kid in the league. When he would stand there everyday, I would say, 'This kid is not going to back down.' I knew then if we were down by one and I'd kick it t out to somebody, he's going to shoot it and he's going to make it."

O'Neal also admitted that he had threatened Bryant he would kill him.

"Ya, I did say that," O'Neal said, prompting Bryant to laugh.

"Of course I remember that day," Bryant said. "I was like, 'Alright, well come on then.'"

The teasing still remained present to this day.

When O'Neal joked his NBA contemporaries may call Bryant "bay-boo" as his wife, Vanessa, does, Bryant responded, "I don't care what they whisper. Bayboo will still drop 60." O'Neal admitted to Bryant he hardly felt thrilled he climbed up ahead to third place on the NBA's all-time scoring list, while O'Neal currently sits at fifth: "I am mad at you about one thing. How the hell did you pass me up in points?" Meanwhile, Bryant relished boasting he eclipsed O'Neal's ring total after he won his fifth NBA championship in 2010. After all, O'Neal bragged after winning his fourth NBA title in 2006 with Miami and repeatedly arguing Bryant could not win without him.

"It pushed me even more," Bryant said. "It drove me even more. When I had five, I wanted to rub it in a little bit."

Bryant later argued that mindset contributed to

their on-court dominance and becoming part of the 2001 NBA championship that went 15-1, which both considered the league's most dominant squad ever. Though the pair disagreed at times over their offensive role, Bryant shared that the two called each other late at night during the playoffs to predetermine which player would dominate the series. Bryant also credited that O'Neal taught him how to lead.

"Shaq is a beast man," Bryant said. "He's smiling all the time when he's on TV and TNT and you see the gregarious personality. But this dude will rip your heart out. That's what I enjoyed about him most was that he was as nasty as I was on the court."

O'Neal later marveled that Bryant shot three air balls his rookie season in the Lakers' Game 5 defeat in Utah in 1997. O'Neal also recalled when he fouled out with 2:33 left in overtime in Game 4 of the 2000 NBA Finals against the Indiana Pacers. Bryant indicated not to worry, proving prophetic that he would carry the team to a win on his own. Bryant made two later jumpers and a tip-in to give the Lakers a 3-1 series lead over Indiana.

"Whatever he said he was going to do from age 18 he was going to do it," O'Neal said. "I knew that from Kobe."

O'Neal asked Bryant to offer some clairvoyance on his upcoming season. But Bryant would not say if this was his last year.

"I'm training and getting ready for the season," said Bryant, whose surgically repaired right shoulder marked his third season-ending injury in consecutive years. "I'm really excited about it because this is my 20th. I'm closer to the end. 20 years is nuts."

Bryant sounded more forthcoming when O'Neal asked him if he considered any of NBA contemporaries to be the so-called "next Kobe Bryant."

Kobe and Shaq's third NBA championship together proved to be their last, with Shaq being the odd-man-out following the 2003-2004 season, when he was traded to the Miami Heat. (L.A. Daily News: Hans Gutknecht)

"Nah. I'm kind of old school," Bryant said. "You have certain players that have that aggressiveness and that mentality. It's tough to tell, man. It's a different generation. I grew up playing against Michael [Jordan] and [Gary Payton] and all these stone-cold assassins. John Stockton and all these guys. So I had that mentality, right. You don't really see that kind of mentality around the league nowadays. Everybody is buddy-buddy and don't want to hurt each other's [feelings]."

Bryant and O'Neal then bemoaned how much less physical the NBA has supposedly become.

"When we play in the Olympics, the physicality in the Olympics has been more physical than the NBA is," Bryant said. "The NBA used to be the toughest and strongest league in the world. Now it's not that. I also don't know what happened to all the seven footers."

O'Neal then interjected, "You know what happened. We killed them all off."

Both Bryant and O'Neal offered a boisterous laugh, a light-hearted moment that juxtaposed the tension they had through all those years playing together from 1996 to 2004. Yet, both have offered public olive branches in recent years. Bryant and O'Neal shared the All-Star MVP in 2009. O'Neal publicly congratulated Bryant for eclipsing Bryant on the NBA's all-time scoring list in 2012. Bryant recorded a video tribute for when the Lakers retired O'Neal's No. 34 jersey in 2013.

And in 2015, Bryant appeared on Shaq's podcast, burying the hatchet, telling old stories and sharing a few laughs. So when O'Neal offered an appreciative goodbye, Bryant answered back with something that may have sounded foreign during their feud.

Said Bryant: "Thank you my man. I appreciate that, brother." ∎

Kobe, Isaiah Rider (center), and Shaq enjoy the parade following their 2001 NBA Finals triumph. (L.A. Daily News: David Sprague)

Kobe's Legacy
Time with Lakers Not Always Smooth, but Memorable
By Vincent Bonsignore • November 29, 2015

The first time I saw Kobe Bryant play basketball he was a 17-year-old kid making his NBA summer league debut at Long Beach State. It was Day 1 of rehearsals for an incredible play which would span two decades, produce five NBA championships, one incredible 81-point scoring night, the construction and implosion of one NBA dynasty and the rebirth of another.

I guess it's only fitting I should now write about closing night.

Bryant announced Sunday he'll retire at the end of the season. Considering the last three injury-ravaged seasons he's endured and the way he's painfully limped around this season, it's the right decision.

We don't have to grimace anymore watching him. From this point on, we can officially just appreciate the last 67 games we get to see one of the greatest of them all.

April will be here before we know it. The final curtain will fall. And one of the greatest Lakers of them all will exit stage left.

As painful as that is to write, it's more comforting knowing we can now just admire him rather than hurt for him.

About that day in Long Beach nearly 20 years ago, Kobe dropped a cold-blooded 27 points on a bunch of grown men.

So yeah, I guess you can say I saw all of this coming. Me and the rest of the sold-out gym getting a glimpse of the kid Jerry West predicted would be the next great NBA superstar.

And boy, oh, boy, did West ever nail it with Kobe.

All you needed was to plant two eyes on the kid with the funny name to understand the greatness West foresaw. It didn't even have to be a trained pair of eyes, either. As long as they were strong enough to peer across the gym, you could tell Kobe played with a purpose and athletic ability that was rare for a 27-year-old veteran, let alone a 17-year-old kid.

We couldn't possibly know about the conviction, the unbending competitiveness, the drive, the determination or the unwillingness to lose. But as we all soon learned, those components were as apparent as all that breathtaking talent wrapped around the slender 6-foot-7 frame.

It was the sword Kobe used to carve up an entire league and make it his own for most of his record-breaking career. And sometimes the curse that would cause static with teammates, coaches and even the Lakers' front office.

From the very beginning, there was give and take with Kobe. Mostly good, but sometimes bad. He was blunt, demanding and he drove a hard bargain with anyone who dared coach him or play with him.

The road wasn't always smooth, the ride not always pleasant.

But it sure was memorable.

I've always said Kobe wrote a script for his life to be the best basketball player who ever lived.

Lakers head coach and Kobe had a tumultuous relationship at times but they thrived together, winning five titles. (San Gabriel Valley Tribune: Keith Birmingham)

It was a noble objective to be sure. And he damn near got there. He fell just short of Michael Jordan, but he put himself in the discussion. And you only have to mention a couple more names before you get to Kobe.

He's top five, easy.

About that script, the problem is he forgot to add other characters.

It was a technical error that sometimes got him in trouble. There was the major falling out with Shaquille O'Neal. He butted heads with Phil Jackson. He went on a infamous rant about Jerry Buss and the Lakers' front office. He wasn't always the warmest teammate. And any Lakers fan will tell you, there were plenty of times you wondered if he even realized there were teammates standing wide open just a few feet away from him.

But as the years unfolded, he was willing to do the necessary re-writes. And by the time Jackson was written back into the script and characters like Pau Gasol, Lamar Odom and Ron Artest were added, Kobe showed us he could be a leading man while also incorporating a great supporting cast.

He was uniquely Los Angeles in that way. The rest of the world gets to see the finished product when the movie credits roll. But the magic isn't on the screen, it's the long, arduous process that goes into taking a simple idea and turning it into a great movie.

As any great script writer will tell you, nailing the ending is always difficult. And as we've seen with Kobe, it can sometimes be clumsy and awkward. The first 15 games made that painfully obvious.

Thankfully Kobe opened the script back up and re-wrote the last scene.

It won't be perfect. He likely won't go out with a playoff run. There will be plenty of more shots that clank off the rim.

But that's OK.

He came to us a skinny kid from Philadelphia.

It's only fitting he'll leave us a middle-aged man, his character arc complete, fulfilling and one of a kind.

All that's left now is to just appreciate him. ∎

Kobe hits a game-tying three, late in the Lakers' Game 2 NBA Finals victory over the Pistons in 2004. It is one of many indelible crunch-time memories that Kobe provided. (L.A. Daily News: Hans Gutknecht)

The Next Challenge

How Will Kobe Handle His Post-NBA Career?

By Mark Medina • January 30, 2016

The words sounded powerful to Kobe Bryant as he heard Michael Jordan gush about his on-court achievements.

Jordan praised Bryant's competitiveness. Jordan complimented Bryant's skills. Jordan highlighted Bryant's influence on the NBA's current generation.

Jordan, the Charlotte Hornets owner, spoke those words in a video tribute in Bryant's final trip to Charlotte last month. It meant a lot to Bryant, who tried to be like Mike with his sharp fundamentals, thirst for championships and demanding personality.

Then, Jordan offered some perspective that could help Bryant with the next chapter once his 20th and final NBA season ends.

"Your next career is going to be something I'm pretty sure you will have to figure out," Jordan said in the video tribute. "From a competitive standpoint, I'm pretty sure you're just like me. You're going to have to find ways to utilize that competitive drive."

The Lakers (9-40) host the Charlotte Hornets (22-25) on Sunday at Staples Center, giving Bryant exactly 33 games before he will have to sweat out those competitive juices elsewhere. For once, Bryant will not try to be like Mike with how he handles his post-NBA career.

Bryant shot down any scenario he would reconsider retirement. Jordan did that twice, which led both to three more NBA titles with the Chicago Bulls (1996-98) and an underwhelming stint with the Washington Wizards (2001-03).

Bryant also ruled out having any ownership, front office or coaching role with any sports team. Jordan oversaw Charlotte's basketball operations in 2006 before becoming the franchise's majority owner in 2010. Jordan has overseen Charlotte making only two NBA playoff appearances and getting swept both times in the first round.

How will Bryant channel his basketball greatness into something else?

"Basketball or whatever sport you play, it comes easy," Bryant said. "You were born and this is what you did at a young age. It's very hard to figure out what the next thing is. But I'll be fine."

Rediscovering a Passion

Bryant and those around him anticipate he will become just as successful in retirement as he did with the Lakers, where he collected five NBA championships and became the franchise's all-time leading scorer.

"He's going to be active," said Chicago Bulls forward Pau Gasol, who won two NBA championships with Bryant on the Lakers (2008-2014). "He's well-positioned to be set and do whatever he wants."

Bryant already has founded Kobe, Inc., a sports-related company that has invested in the Body Armor

Kobe Bryant answers questions about the state of the Lakers during a press conference before welcoming campers to his Kobe Basketball Academy at UCSB, in July 2013. Kobe became refreshingly open with the media late in his career. (L.A. Daily News: Michael Owen Baker)

sports drink. Bryant's company has also trademarked various phrases, including "Friends Hang Sometimes, Banners Hang Forever." Bryant also has committed toward traveling to China and Africa, trips that could include promoting his Nike brand and hosting basketball clinics.

After producing his "Muse" documentary that aired on Showtime last year, a camera crew has followed Bryant throughout his final NBA season in what could turn into another documentary. When Bryant announced his retirement on Nov. 29, 2015, Bryant called himself "a storyteller." Bryant also described himself as "extremely passionate" and "obsessive" about that craft.

"I've been very fortunate enough to find it to the point that it keeps me up at night," Bryant said. "I'm constantly working, studying and trying to get better at it."

That surprises no one.

"He's going to work at that just like he worked at his game," Lakers coach Byron Scott said. "Whatever he's involved in is going to be successful because he's going to put the time and the effort to make it that way."

Handling His Competitive Urge

But can that fully replace Bryant's love for basketball?

"I don't know," said former Lakers center and current TNT analyst Shaquille O'Neal, who has publicly made amends with Bryant after their contentious relationship during their eight years together (1996-2004). "It's going to be difficult. You wake up and you don't have anything to do."

Bryant will have plenty to do, but it will not involve him dominating opponents on the basketball court. After admitting he "would have loved to play overseas

for a season," Bryant changed his sentiments nearly a month ago. He conceded, "my body won't let me." Bryant and those around him strongly doubt he will play pickup games at local gyms just to satisfy his hoops fix.

"I'm always going to be working. I can't stop," Bryant said. "I have too much energy. I'm always going to be really, really working really, really hard. The hardest thing is going to be to sit down and relax."

So even if Bryant has sounded at peace with coaches, teammates and reporters throughout his final NBA season, he has anticipated feeling a sudden dread of finality.

"I'm waiting for it to really hit heavy," Bryant said. "Right now, I feel really good. It's really smooth. But it can't be that smooth. I'm walking away from the game that I've been playing since I was two years old. At some point, it has to hit like a ton of bricks. I'm on pins and needles to see if that will happen." Former Lakers general manager and Golden State Warriors executive Jerry West predicted that will happen fairly soon.

"I will guarantee you after a year," West said. "The thing with being competitive, he also has to be disciplined. All of a sudden, you're going to have to find a way to be disciplined with your life."

That led Scott to joke Bryant may want to take up golf "so he can have that competitive flow still going." But it sounds like Bryant already has planned for that. He recently told SiriusXM NBA Radio he wants to stay physically active during his post-NBA career.

Bryant plans to still wake up as early as 6 a.m. for weight-training workouts. Bryant said he would like to take up skiing, surfing and sky diving for the first time. Former tennis star Pete Sampras has also offered to give Bryant lessons.

Kobe expects the legendary passion and focus he displayed on the court to extend to his post-playing career business and creative endeavors. (L.A. Daily News: Michael Owen Baker)

"I'll continue to stay in good shape," Bryant said. "It's important from a health perspective and also to maintain a schedule. To have a career end and you feel like it would be more fun and more free to be able to wake up and not have a schedule and things of that sort? If anything, I think that makes things more confusing."

Sacramento Kings forward and former Lakers teammate Caron Butler no longer sounded confused after having private conversations with Bryant over dinner last month before his final game in Sacramento.

In addition toward having more time to spend with his wife (Vanessa) and daughters (Natalia, Gianna), Bryant also outlined to Butler a full itinerary that will keep himself distracted enough not to worry about not holding, dribbling and shooting a ball.

"He's going to be extremely busy," said Butler, who's considered one of Bryant's closest friends. "I'm really happy for him. The transition is going to be smooth because he has so much going on. He's going to be occupied with his projects."

Savoring the Moment

With some time left before his last NBA game on April 13 against Utah at Staples Center, Bryant listened intently to a message from his idol last month. Unlike in years past, it did not involve trash talk, advice on how to score or insight on how to elevate his teammates. Instead, Jordan offered an olive branch on how to succeed away from the hardwood.

"I look forward toward seeing what you do next," Jordan said in the video tribute. "If you ever need anything, you have my number. Stay in touch." ■

Kobe Bryant was one-of-a-kind in his brilliant 20-year NBA career and truly a Laker for life. (San Gabriel Valley Tribune: Keith Birmingham)

LOS ANGELES NEWS GROUP

Pasadena Star-News
San Gabriel Valley Tribune
Whittier Daily News

Los Angeles Daily News

DAILY BREEZE

PRESS-TELEGRAM

Redlands Daily Facts

Pasadena Star-News

INLAND VALLEY
DAILY BULLETIN

THE SUN

Local Brand Leaders — Known and Trusted for Over 100 Years

As premium local content providers, each of the LANG newspapers has a long history of editorial excellence in their own respective markets — forming a special kind of trust and brand loyalty that readers really value. Exclusive local content sets the Los Angeles News Group apart, providing readers and users with news and information they won't find anywhere else. From local elections to their home team's top scores, when area residents need late-breaking news, LANG newspapers, websites and mobile media are their number one resource.